PIANO • VOCAL • GUITAR

W9-DFK-083

The BIG BANDS

Theme Songs & Top Hits

Articles by Jeff Sultanof

ISBN 0-7935-4576-5

HAL•LEONARD®
CORPORATION
7777 W. BLUEMOUND RD. P.O. BOX 13819 MILWAUKEE, WI 53213

Contents

THE BIG BANDS
Alphabetically by Song Title

Contents
THE BIG BANDS
Alphabetically by Big Band

The Band's Official Theme Song

In the late 1930s and early 1940s big band music was all over the airwaves. The sounds of these jumping, massed ensembles filled the jukeboxes and record stores. Live appearances would usually fill ballrooms, college dance halls and theatres between movie features. The music the bands played was often the top songs of the era, composed by American geniuses like Jerome Kern, George Gershwin, Johnny Mercer, Cole Porter and Duke Ellington. Jitterbug was the most popular dance of the day, a response to the jivey swing beat. There were hot, lively, more jazz-oriented bands, like Benny Goodman, for the fans of serious swing. There were the bands that offered quieter, more sentimental sounds, called 'sweet bands' in the trade. And some bands relied on novelty numbers, even gimmicks, for their appeal.

It was an era when the golden age of popular songwriting in America was at its apex, with hundreds of songs that have become standards the world over—"Body and Soul," "Begin the Beguine," "Heart and Soul," "Bewitched," and "All the Things You Are," just to name a few. It was a time when the art of arranging music for saxes, brass and rhythm reached a high point, creating sounds uniquely American, which are now studied and analyzed in college classrooms all over the world. Singers such as Frank Sinatra, Peggy Lee, Dick Haymes and Doris Day became stars with bands, taking the vocal style of popular song into a new age. Vocal groups singing with bands such as the Fred Waring Glee Club, The Pied Pipers, The Modernaires and The Beachcombers, set the standard for American popular choral music in terms of diction, sonic blend and presentation. Employment for skilled musicians was at an all-time high. The art of jazz improvisation flourished more than ever with the sounds of Benny Goodman, Lester Young, Jimmy Blanton, Johnny Hodges, Bunny Berigan, Benny Carter and a host of others. It was understood that the great soloists in American music of the '30s and '40s were either members of the bands, or got their starts playing in them. Dizzy Gillespie and Gerry Mulligan have often stated that their years of big band playing were invaluable, and both became respected leaders themselves in later years.

All in all, the effects of the era are still reverberating in popular, jazz and even the modern classical music of today.

Beginnings

The Paul Whiteman Orchestra, 1923

Interestingly, it took about sixteen years for the big band era to arrive. As with any popular music, the roots were there for years waiting for the right combination of circumstances, the right sound, and the right personality to kick it off. Dance music, of course, has always been with us in some form, and dance orchestras were always popular for social events. The saxophone became an instrument perfect for dance music, because of its volume, its sound that could blend with almost any other instrument, and its emotionally charged, near-vocal ability to bring a modern popular song to life. (It was also easy to learn.) When a song was published in the early 20th century, the publisher usually provided arrangements for any number and combination of instruments, but because these arrangements were so generic, they had no real personality of their own. In 1913, Art Hickman put together one of the first professional dance bands featuring arrangements specifically written for his players. Paul Whiteman followed suit in 1919, with the additional idea of actual concerts (Whiteman commissioned Gershwin to write "Rhapsody in Blue" to be premiered in Carnegie Hall in 1924), and his band went on to sell millions of records, appear on radio programs, and tour extensively. After his success, many bands were formed to meet the sudden demand throughout the country. Some, like Whiteman's and Hal Kemp's early band, went overseas to great acclaim. In New York, Fletcher Henderson was playing important engagements by the early '20s. His arranger Don Redman proved a major influence by dividing the band up into saxophone and brass choirs, often playing these sections against one another (call-and-response), that became a popular technique for many years. Duke Ellington's band at the Kentucky Club went another way. His band featured adventurous harmonies, unusual instrumental combinations and musical effects that his promoters liked to call 'jungle music' — wa-wa and growling brass, and loud, raucous reeds. Even though he played his share of current hits, Ellington was also one of the first bandleaders to feature his own compositions. In Detroit, classical pianist Jean Goldkette formed a legendary band with Bix Beiderbecke, Frank Trumbauer and Bill Challis, and it was incredibly popular among the young college crowd that loved hot music. Also popular in the 1920s college circuit was Ben Pollack's band, which included future leaders such as Benny Goodman, Glenn Miller and Jack Teagarden. In California, Gus Arnheim filled the Cocoanut Grove nightly with his dance music.

The Great Depression

By the late '20s, there were hundreds of bands touring the country, recording and broadcasting, and the public loved them. The depression that began with the stock market crash in October of 1929 changed everything. Suddenly, the average man had trouble getting a job or getting food for his family. Money for dances or records was hard to come by. Without this kind of support, the current bands were doomed. Some bands, such as the Casa Loma band, flourished during those years on radio broadcasts, but many others, particularly the bands playing the hamlets of the midwest and the south, often found themselves stranded on the road. The great Bennie Moten band, with future bandleader Count Basie on piano, arrived at a recording session in near starvation. Groups finally had to disband. The music that the public wanted to hear in the first couple of years of the depression was sweet, gentle and sentimental. The Guy Lombardo, Jan Garber, Eddy Duchin, Hal Kemp and Leo Reisman orchestras were what they seemed to want. Other leaders had gimmicks. Clyde McCoy turned "Sugar Blues" into a talking-trumpet novelty that sustained him and his band for many years, as did Henry Busse with his specialty, "Hot Lips." Cab Calloway, Chick Webb

and other black jazz-oriented groups plodded on for whatever was available, often touring in the deep south, where conditions for travel were deplorable.

The Craze Begins

Benny Goodman and orchestra, the breakthrough swing band.

With Franklin Roosevelt as president beginning in 1933, the mood of the country changed. People felt that they had something to hope for, that conditions would improve. The time was ripe for a new style of music to reflect these new feelings of positivism. As early as 1934, surveys showed that the most popular form of radio entertainment was dance music. With the National Biscuit Company as the sponsor, NBC radio premiered the "Let's Dance" program. Three bands were presented over a weekly three hour program which ran for twenty-six weeks. It was a huge success, and many music lovers across the country heard Benny Goodman's new band, playing arrangements by pioneer bandleader Fletcher Henderson. Still, when Benny and band played their new brand of hot swing across the country in 1935, his music was often met with disdain and downright hostility. The band was reduced to playing stock arrangements in order to hold on to jobs.

It was in California, at the Palomar in Pismo Beach on August 21, 1935, to be exact, that the first intimations of a national craze were first experienced. Benny's repertoire of Fletcher Henderson swing met with wild applause for the first time in a public dance engagement in a ballroom. Benny was stunned. An extended job at the Congress Hotel in Chicago provided many broadcasts, excellent publicity, coverage in the print media, and increased record sales. The band started winning important polls in music magazines. The Big Band Era finally came of age when Goodman played the Paramount Theatre in New York. On his opening show on March 3, 1937, the band was met with a theatre full of screaming, hysterical, clapping and shouting fans. During the show, many couples jitterbugged in the aisles. That first day, the Paramount reported 21,000 paid admissions. The resulting publicity was reported all over the world. January 16, 1938 provided the icing on the cake, a sold-out crowd for Goodman's concert at Carnegie Hall.

By 1938, swing music was all over the place. Artie Shaw's classic record of Cole Porter's "Begin the Beguine," a song that was first heard on Broadway in 1935 and then forgotten, made Shaw a superstar. Charlie Barnet, who'd been around for years playing dance jobs, became a star himself with his version of Ray Noble's "Cherokee." Count Basie's band from Kansas City was promoted by writer and activist John Hammond, and its booking at the Famous Door on 52nd Street in New York helped to make it a sensation. Jimmie Lunceford's exciting band was featuring arrangements by the now legendary arranger Sy Oliver, and became the ultimate attraction for live shows. (Glenn Miller thought their stage show the best he'd ever seen, and many of his own band's visual routines were patterned on Lunceford's.) Chick Webb was now firmly ensconced at the Savoy Ballroom in Harlem, where he won many a "battle of bands," beating out Benny Goodman himself. Duke Ellington became more popular than ever, especially since many bands were playing his music as well as their own.

One of the ways a band could be established, besides a hit record, was an important booking at a major ballroom, often resulting in radio broadcasts. A summer engagement at the Glen Island Casino in New York was a sure-fire attention-getter. Glenn Miller was the band featured during the 1939 summer season, and his broadcasts and records such as "In the Mood" were the beginning of a phenomenally successful career. In 1941, the Claude Thornhill band similarly gained important coast-to-coast publicity from broadcasts emanating from Glen Island Casino. Wayne King became so identified with the Aragon Ballroom in Chicago that he played there the night before it closed forever in 1964.

Bands in the 1940s

By the 1940s, sidemen who'd become stars left to form their own ensembles. Harry James made his name with Benny Goodman's outfit, and, in 1939, went out on his own with a band that included a skinny singer named Frank Sinatra. Lionel Hampton, another Goodman alumnus, started his own successful orchestra in 1940. Freddie Slack, who'd been the pianist in both the Jimmy Dorsey and Will Bradley-Ray McKinley bands, had a hit record, "Cow-Cow Boogie," almost as soon as he started his own group. Sonny Dunham and Frankie Carle also fronted popular ensembles after having established themselves with other leaders.

Some big bands had their biggest hits after many years in the field. Jimmy Dorsey worked the best hotels and theatres, but his 1941 hit records of "Green Eyes" and "Amapola" made him a bigger star than ever. Brother Tommy Dorsey had a number of hits in the '30s such as "Marie" and "Song of India." But his band of the early '40s rose to new levels of popularity. With Frank Sinatra and The Pied Pipers handling the vocals, Tommy recorded the song "I'll Never Smile Again." The record was a number one song for twelve weeks in 1940, and remains one of the greatest hits of the big band era. Les Brown's band received a major shot in the arm with the arrival of seventeen-year-old Doris Day handling the vocals. She left the band soon after she joined in 1941, but she returned in 1945 to make such classic recordings as "Sentimental Journey" and "Till the End of Time."

The war years were a time of major change in the music business. As early as 1941, the bands felt the effects of the draft when key members were forced to leave for the service. By 1942, it was not unusual to replace an entire section of musicians almost overnight. Travel restrictions, gas shortages, a 20% amusement tax on ballrooms, and midnight curfews forced groups to disband and ballrooms to close. But perhaps the biggest blow was a recording ban imposed by the musician's union in 1942. Concerned that musicians were not being paid when their recordings were played on the radio and in jukeboxes, union boss James Petrillo forbade union members to record until the record labels signed a new agreement establishing a recording tax. Decca signed the agreement in 1943, but RCA and Columbia held out until 1944. There were few new recordings of big bands, except special records called V-Discs made for the armed forces and unavailable to the general public. New recordings were being made, but they starred singers with a cappella choral accompaniment—the very singers who got their starts with the big bands. In just a short time, the star singers would be monopolizing the airwaves as solo acts.

By the time World War II ended, the returning vets were anxious to get on with their lives, raise families and buy homes. Times had changed. Singing stars like Frank Sinatra and Doris Day ruled the airwaves with ballads. Many historians place the year 1946 as the end of the Big Band Era, yet there was still a strong audience for the ensembles, and 1946 through 1950 was one of the richest periods for some bands musically. Woody Herman, who'd been leading a band since 1936, led one of the finest bands of his career in 1945, which was subsequently called the first "herd." It was also a popular band, with its own radio show, best-selling records, and frequent broadcasts. Stan Kenton's career soared after several tough years of getting established. He called his music "Artistry in Rhythm." Later on, calling his music "Progressive Jazz," he played both dances and concerts to a wildly enthusiastic public. Ray McKinley not only played pop novelty songs (often singing them himself), he let composer/arranger Eddie Sauter compose some of the most complex and interesting music of that time.

During the war years, a new style of jazz emerged that was later given the name "bebop." Originally conceived as small-group music, several big bands played in the bebop style. Billy Eckstine was one of the first, and the band featured many musicians who would later become stars of the new music. Dizzy Gillespie's was the first big band to play modern jazz in Europe, sharply dividing the jazz fraternity in France. Claude Thornhill's band was taught the new music by arrangers Gil Evans and Gerry Mulligan, and the famous Miles Davis nonet of 1949-50 was a direct outgrowth of the Thornhill ensemble. Even Woody Herman and Benny Goodman led bands that played more modern sounds, but, unfortunately, these bands did not last long.

The 1950s and Beyond

"Will the big bands ever come back?" was an oft-repeated phrase in the early '50s, a period when the radio hits were often commercial novelty songs, a far cry from the substantial swing of the late '30s and early '40s. Many big groups had long since disbanded, but many others, like Harry James, Tommy Dorsey, Count Basie and Duke Ellington were still on the road playing hotels and the ballrooms that were still in operation. The quick ascent of rock 'n' roll in 1955 made big band music seem a thing of the past. But rock 'n' roll did not completely kill swing music. The advent of television kept many people at home, but new bands were on the music scene, and some of them became very successful. Ray Anthony eventually got his own television show. Of course, one of the biggest successes in television was a show hosted by a man who'd been on the road for years. Lawrence Welk's show was on the ABC network for sixteen years, then in syndication for more years on the air, and he became a multi-millionaire. Les Elgart's band was one of the most popular on the college prom circuit. Billy May's studio recordings were so popular that he was convinced to take a band on the road. After two years, however, Sam Donahue took over the leadership and Billy went back to the Hollywood studios. Johnny Richards' band was initially financed by Stan Kenton. He kept it going off and on until his death with little financial success. Quincy Jones led a fabulous ensemble, but increasing responsibilities as a record company executive forced him to give it up.

Will the big bands ever come back? In a sense, they've never left. CD reissues of the bands fill the record stores, and some have even been digitally remastered. There are fewer places for them to play, but that has not stopped such ensembles led by Thad Jones and Mel Lewis, Maynard Ferguson, Bob Mintzer, John and Alec Dankworth, Tom Talbert, and Illinois Jacquet. The Glenn Miller, Count Basie, Woody Herman and Tommy Dorsey orchestras work regularly, and hundreds of jazz ensembles in high schools and colleges play and study music new and old. The hippest of Generation X seem to have discovered hot swing music. Many people of all ages from all over the world realize that big band music is part of America's musical heritage. Every day, some young person hears a big band and gets turned on to the beauty and power of saxophones and brass.

At any given moment, somewhere in the world a big band is swinging away. May it ever be so!

PROFILES OF SELECTED BANDLEADERS

Ray Anthony

Theme Song: The Man with the Horn *(featured in this collection)*
Hit Recordings: Slaughter on Tenth Avenue, Count Every Star, Harbor Lights, At Last, The Hokey Pokey, The Bunny Hop, Dragnet

Ray Anthony led a very popular big band in the 1950s, an era when big bands were not as popular as singing stars, rhythm & blues, and rock 'n' roll. He was born in Bentleyville, Pennsylvania in 1922, and grew up in Cleveland, Ohio. He was given a trumpet by his father at the age of five and played with the family band. Anthony later joined the trumpet sections of the Al Donahue, Glenn Miller and Jimmy Dorsey bands. During World War II he enlisted in the Navy and was part of the entertainment section of the Great Lakes Naval Station. After the war he formed his own dance band back in Cleveland. By 1949, his manager, Fred Benson, was convinced that Anthony's band had an opportunity to be a national attraction. He was proven correct, as Anthony's records consistently placed in the top ten music charts. In 1953, his version of "Dragnet" became a million seller. In that year, he and his band were the summer replacement TV show for Perry Como's "Chesterfield Supper Club." In 1957, Anthony hosted a variety show on ABC television. Ray's group disbanded in 1960, and he opened a lounge act at the Sahara Hotel in Las Vegas — a top attraction for twenty years. In 1980, Anthony formed another band which still tours at this writing.

Gus Arnheim

Theme Song: Sweet and Lovely *(featured in this collection)*
Hit Recordings: So Rare, Sleepy Valley, Go Home and Tell Your Mother, I Surrender, The Little Things in Life

Gus Arnheim and the Cocoanut Grove restaurant were synonymous in the late '20s to early '30s. His was one of the most successful bands in the west coast during this period. Arnheim was born in 1898 and got his early start as a pianist with the pioneering west coast group Abe Lyman and His Californians. When he left Lyman in 1926, his new band opened at the Ambassador Hotel's Cocoanut Grove to immediate fame. Most of the young Hollywood stars met to eat and dance at the Grove, and Arnheim packed the room nightly. Because his group was so visible by the Hollywood community, someone singing with his band could become a star overnight. Bing Crosby credits his exposure with the Arnheim band as the first important step in his solo career. Others who made an early reputation singing with Arnheim were Russ Columbo, Shirley Ross, Donald Novis, The Sportsmen and Andy Russell. By 1936, Arnheim decided to modernize the band's style, and brought in jazz legend Budd Johnson to write the arrangements. He also made future bandleader Stan Kenton the assistant conductor. The experiment was a failure and Arnheim soon returned to his sweet dance band sounds. After the war, he gave up the band to write for and lead orchestras for motion pictures and television. He died in Beverly Hills in 1955.

Desi Arnaz

Theme Song: Cuban Pete *(featured in this collection)*
Hit Recordings:: Babalu, Carnival in Rio, El Cumbanchero

Desi Arnaz, née Desiderio Alberto Arnaz y de Acha III, was born on March 2, 1917, in Cuba. His family possessed wealth and property, and young Desiderio was destined to become a lawyer and a politician like his father. In 1933, Desi's father was arrested and his property confiscated during the first Batista revolution. The boy and his mother escaped to Florida. After working at miscellaneous jobs in Miami, Arnaz auditioned for the Siboney Septet at the Roney Plaza Hotel in Miami Beach. A year later he became a featured singer with the king of Latin music, Xavier Cugat. He was leading his own band at New York's La Conga Club, where he was spotted by Larry Hart of the team Rodgers and Hart. Desi joined the cast of the show *Too Many Girls* in 1939, and he became a sensation overnight. He was asked to repeat his role in the film version of the show (released in 1940), and met future wife Lucille Ball on the set. After the war, he reorganized his band, and, thanks to a successful opening engagement at Ciro's in Los Angeles, it became a smash. The band toured all across the country in ballrooms and theatres to large crowds, and made a series of exciting records for RCA. He disbanded when he and Lucy decided to bring a situation comedy to television, a little show called "I Love Lucy." Arnaz became head of the Desilu empire, and later was divorced from Lucille Ball. He died in California in 1986.

Charlie Barnet

Theme Song: Redskin Rhumba
Hit Recordings:
Cherokee *(featured in this collection)*, Pompton Turnpike, Where Was I?, I Hear a Rhapsody, Skyliner

Born in New York in 1913, Barnet started his first band over the objections of his wealthy family. The band opened in 1933 at the Paramount Grill. From the very beginning, Barnet led a group that included both black and white musicians, something quite daring at the time. The band was somewhat successful for the next six years. In 1939, on a trip to the RCA studios for a record date, arranger/trumpeter Billy May passed out the parts to a tune that the Barnet band was to record that day. The response by the recording director was underwhelming, yet, upon the tune's release, "Cherokee" became one of the most popular records of the entire big band era. Barnet's band became a major attraction overnight, and it remained so until he disbanded in 1949. Charlie loved Duke Ellington, and many of his recordings showed his love of Duke's musical style. Barnet was also good at spotting and encouraging talented players and singers, and his band's members included such future stars as Lena Horne, Kay Starr, Eddie Sauter, Skip Martin, Frances Wayne, Neal Hefti, and Doc Severinsen. In 1966, after years of semi-retirement, Barnet led his last band for personal appearances in California and New York. It was a tribute to him that this was one of the finest bands he ever led.

Count Basie

Theme Song: One O'Clock Jump
Hit Recordings: Alright, Okay, You Win *(featured in this collection)*; All of Me; Jimmy's Blues; Jivin' Joe Jackson; The Mad Boogie; Open the Door, Richard!

He was born William Basie in New Jersey in 1904. He started piano lessons with his mother, and informally studied piano with Fats Waller and other pianists of the Harlem stride style. Beginning in his teens Basie toured the vaudeville circuits as a pianist and music director. During one of these tours he was stranded in Kansas City in 1927, and decided to stay there, at first playing in silent theatres. The young man began playing in local bands there, finally forming his own band in 1935 under the name the Barons of Rhythm, and securing a long term engagement at the Reno Club in Kansas City. Radio broadcasts brought the band fame, and by 1936 the expanded version was now called the Count Basie Orchestra. Hit recordings soon followed, particularly "One O'Clock Jump," "Jumpin' at the Woodside," and "Taxi War Dance." Basie's group was musically on the cutting edge in the swing era, with a forward-looking improvisational jazz style. The band was known as having the best rhythm section in the business, with Basie on piano. Except for two years in the early 1950s, Basie kept a band together for more than forty years. He was one of the great jazz pianists of the century, one whose playing in trios and ensembles particularly is held as the model for all aspiring jazz pianists. Basie's influence on other big bands, as well as practically all jazz musicians, cannot be overestimated. He died in Hollywood in 1984.

Bunny Berigan

Theme Song: I Can't Get Started with You *(featured in this collection)*
Hit Recordings: The Prisoner's Song, The First Time I Saw You, I Cried for You

Berigan was born in 1908 in Fox Lake, Wisconsin. He initially took up the violin, but started playing trumpet at the age of eleven. He became one of the most beloved musicians of his generation. Other top musicians discovered his talent when he was barely in his twenties, and his solos graced such bands as Hal Kemp, Abe Lyman, Paul Whiteman, Benny Goodman, and Tommy Dorsey. Berigan started his own band in 1937, and soon had a tremendous hit with the Vernon Duke-Ira Gershwin song "I Can't Get Started with You," in which he not only played solo, but sang a chorus of the tune. The recording was also notable as one of the few pop records that was released on a twelve-inch disc. Berigan's band was not the commercial success it should have been, and he had to break it up in 1940. Tommy Dorsey immediately offered him his old job, and soon Berigan was blowing incredible solos in the Dorsey band. But in 1941, he was fronting another band of his own. This edition was also a failure, but undaunted, Berigan put together yet another one. By this time he was an ill man, and he passed away on

June 2, 1942 at the age of thirty-four. Berigan immediately became legendary as one of the great trumpet stylists in the history of jazz and American music. His solos are still studied by trumpet players worldwide, and his recordings are as popular as ever.

Will Bradley

Theme Songs: Think of Me (opener), Strange Cargo (closer)
Hit Recordings: Beat Me Daddy, Eight to the Bar *(featured in this collection);* In the Hall of the Mountain King; Scrub Me Mama with a Boogie Beat; High on a Windy Hill

Born Wilbur Schwichtenburg in 1912, Bradley was an in-demand trombonist for record dates and radio orchestras when agent Willard Alexander told him that his agency would back him as a bandleader. Alexander brought Bradley together with drummer Ray McKinley. Even though both musicians admired and respected each other, Bradley wanted to have a ballad-based group featuring his trombone, and McKinley wanted to play swing. When the band's recording of "Beat Me Daddy, Eight to the Bar" became a hit, the band's style changed to boogie-woogie. McKinley realized that boogie-woogie was the band's ticket to major success, but Bradley was unhappy emphasizing the style. Things came to a head, and in 1942, McKinley left to form his own band. Bradley continued, but soon had to disband when the draft took six of his musicians overnight. He returned to studio work, where he was in demand until he retired in the 1960s. In addition to his trombone playing, he was a respected composer of contemporary concert music.

Les Brown

(Les Brown and the Band of Renown)

Theme Songs: Dance of the Blue Devils, Leap Frog (*featured in this collection*), Sentimental Journey (*featured in this collection*)

Hit Recordings: Joltin' Joe DiMaggio, 'Tis Autumn, My Dreams are Getting Better All the Time, I've Got My Love to Keep Me Warm, Till the End of Time

Lester Raymond Brown was born in 1912. His principal instrument is saxophone. Unlike most of the other musicians of the swing era, Brown studied music formally, first at Ithaca College (where he studied with Wallingford Riegger), and also at New York Military Academy and Duke University. He formed his first dance band at Duke in 1934, the Blue Devils, and toured with them until most of the band went back to the college to complete their degrees. Brown free-lanced in New York, arranged for the Isham Jones, Jimmy Dorsey, Larry Clinton and Red Nichols bands until he started another orchestra in 1938. The group was relatively popular, but received a considerable boost when a young singer joined the band in August of 1940. Seventeen-year-old Doris Day was a sensation, but she only remained with the band for a year. Brown soon acquired saxophonist/novelty singer Butch Stone, and the band's reviews and record sales became stronger and stronger. Brown's biggest hit came when Doris Day returned to the band for some recordings in 1945, and "Sentimental Journey" has been identified with her ever since. Brown disbanded in 1946, forgetting that he had a contract to play at the Hollywood Palladium in March of 1947. The Palladium management would not allow him to cancel, so he put together a new band. Along the way, he became Bob Hope's musical director and remained one of the busiest bandleaders in the west coast. Now semi-retired, he can still be found fronting a wonderful band at Disneyland or in a recording studio.

Frankie Carle

Theme Song: Sunrise Serenade (*featured in this collection*)

Hit Recordings: A Little on the Lonely Side, Oh! What It Seemed to Be, Rumors Are Flying, Beg Your Pardon, Cruising Down the River

Carle (born 1903) was a successful pianist/composer before he started his own outfit in 1944. In show business since 1918, he made his early reputation playing piano with the Mal Hallett Orchestra. He eventually joined the Horace Heidt band, and was so popular a personality and performer that he became co-leader of that organization by 1943. But Carle wanted his own outfit, and with Heidt's blessing, Frankie's new band opened in New York. He was a favorite at many hotels, ballrooms and theatres for many years thereafter, and he continued to compose hit songs. One of them, "Oh! What It Seemed to Be" featured a wonderful new singer named Marjorie Hughes. When the record went to number one on the Hit Parade, it was reported that Marjorie was actually Frankie's daughter. In the mid '50s, Carle disbanded and formed a touring act called Frankie Carle and His Girlfriends, which appeared in Las Vegas and Lake Tahoe.

Xavier Cugat

Theme Song: My Shawl (*featured in this collection*)

Hit Recordings: Say Si Si, Night Must Fall, Perfidia, Brazil

A great personality who personified Latin music for most Americans, Cugat was born in 1900 in Barcelona. He grew up in Cuba, first coming to the U.S. at a young age. He had been a violinist with Anson Weeks and Phil Harris when he put together a group to play at the Waldorf Astoria Hotel in New York in 1933. The Waldorf soon became Cugat's New York headquarters. Cugat's band received a major shot in the arm when it was chosen to be one of the orchestras on the national radio program "Let's Dance," a three hour once-a-week extravaganza which also propelled Benny Goodman's orchestra to prominence. He appeared in many motion pictures and continued to play his style of rhythmic Latin music throughout the 1960s. He launched the careers of singer Abbe Lane in the '50s and singer/guitarist Charo in the '70s, both of whom were at one time Mrs. Cugat. Xavier died in 1990.

Jimmy Dorsey

Theme Song:
Contrasts
Hit Recordings:
Amapola (Pretty Little Poppy) *(featured in this collection)*, Green Eyes, Blue Champagne, Besame Mucho, The Breeze and I, So Rare

In addition to being one of the great clarinet and alto saxophone virtuosos, among the big band leaders, Dorsey led one of the most popular orchestras in the country. He was born in 1904 and was given early instruction in music by his father. Jimmy and younger brother Tommy soon built extensive reputations for themselves in the music world, playing with The California Ramblers, Red Nichols and Paul Whiteman. The brothers decided to form their own orchestra in 1934. Their records and ballroom appearances were very popular, but Jimmy and Tommy fought continuously. Finally, after a disagreement over the tempo of a song, Tommy walked out, leaving Jimmy with his own band. It took until 1941 for Jimmy to break into the the big money with such recordings as "Amapola" and "Green Eyes." Vocalists Bob Eberly and Helen O'Connell were the key elements of Jimmy's success. Bob Eberly was Frank Sinatra's role model, a fact that Sinatra himself acknowledged. In many ways, however, Dorsey's later 1944-48 band was one of the best he ever led, playing arrangements by future Sinatra producer Sonny Burke, and featuring such excellent musicians as Charlie Teagarden, Skip Layton, and Conrad Gozzo, one of the great lead

trumpeters of all time. Jimmy rejoined his brother's band as a featured performer in 1953. He died in March of 1957, a year after Tommy.

Tommy Dorsey

Theme Song:
I'm Getting Sentimental over You
Hit Recordings:
Let's Get Away From It All; Marie *(both featured in this collection)*; Boogie Woogie, You; Music, Maestro, Please; All the Things You Are; Dolores; There Are Such Things, and many others.

Tommy was born in 1905. Along with brother Jimmy, he played with some of the finest dance and jazz orchestras of the '20s and '30s. He and Jimmy started their own band in 1934, but the partnership ended when Tommy walked out one evening during an engagement at Glen Island Casino. Tommy quickly took over a band led by arranger Joe Haymes and built a legendary ensemble, one that big band historian George Simon called "the greatest all-round dance band of them all." It consistently placed high in music magazine polls in both the sweet and swing categories. Throughout its long history, Dorsey's band included such excellent musicians as Buddy Rich, Bunny Berigan, Skeets Herfurt, Dave Tough, Ziggy Elman and Buddy DeFranco. It featured the vocal talents of Jack Leonard, Frank Sinatra, Jo Stafford, Lynn Roberts, The Pied Pipers, The Sentimentalists and The Beachcombers. Dorsey had a brilliant arranging staff of Paul Weston, Axel Stordahl, Bill Finegan, Nelson Riddle and Sy Oliver. And above all, the band had Tommy's trombone, one of the most distinctive and gorgeous sounds of the entire era, still studied and admired by both classical and jazz performers. Eventually Tommy set up his own music publishing company, owned his own ballroom (The Casino Gardens, in which two of the partners were Harry James and brother Jimmy), and set up his own booking office. Economic conditions forced him to disband in 1946, but he formed another band and was back touring by 1948. When his brother rejoined the ensemble in 1953, the band was still quite busy and popular, particularly at New York's Statler Hotel, and on the television show "Stage Show," produced by Jackie Gleason. Tommy died in November of 1956, but the band is still out on the road, led by trombonist Buddy Morrow at this writing.

Sonny Dunham

Theme Song: Memories of You *(featured in this collection)*
Hit Recordings: Come and Get It

One of the great trumpet stars of the swing era was Sonny (Elmer) Dunham, born in 1914. He was a featured performer on trombone with Ben Bernie. He switched to trumpet when he joined the Paul Tremaine outfit. He later joined the Casa Loma Orchestra in 1932, where his blazing virtuoso style made their version of "Memories of You" a standout. After forming a short-lived band in 1937, he returned to Casa Loma, but obviously bandleading was in his blood, for he started his own group again in 1940. This band was popular for several years, appearing in several motion pictures. Dunham himself was a funny, articulate musician who was so self-effacing that critics complained the band was "too cool" and uninvolving. It featured some wonderful musicians, such as Pete Candoli, Corky Corcoran, Ray Kellogg, and arrangements by George (The Fox) Williams. All of these talents rose to prominence after they left Dunham. Sonny gave the band up in 1951, moved to Florida and continued to play and lead bands for steamship excursions. He retired from the business in 1984.

Billy Eckstine

Hit Recordings: A Cottage for Sale *(featured in this collection)*, Prisoner of Love, I'm in the Mood for Love, You Call It Madness (But I Call It Love)

Eckstine was discovered by tenor saxophonist-arranger Budd Johnson and joined the Earl Hines band in 1939. In 1944 he started his own big band. His musical directors were Johnson and Dizzy Gillespie. Eckstine's female vocalist was Sarah Vaughan. Some of the musicians that played in the band at one time or another were Charlie Parker, Dexter Gordon, Art Blakey, Miles Davis, Fats Navarro, Lucky Thompson and Gene Ammons. So why wasn't the band the resounding success that everyone in the jazz world thought it would be? The band's recordings were one factor. Eckstine's releases for the National label were recorded so poorly that they did not receive the airplay they deserved. Another factor was the band's style, a brand of modern jazz that was so new that the music turned off many of the fans coming to hear Eckstine sing. Billy tried hard for three years to make the format work, but eventually he succumbed to the pressures of his booking agents and became a solo attraction. He was one of the first artists to sign with MGM records, who promoted him heavily and made him the star that he remained until his death in 1993. In the '70s, the release of live recordings made for the Armed Forces Jubilee program in 1945 proved how good the band was, and further illustrated how it was ahead of its time.

Les Elgart

Theme Song: The Dancing Sound
Hit Recordings: Bandstand Boogie *(featured in this collection)*, Sophisticated Swing

Les Elgart was born in 1918. He was a skilled trumpet player who had excellent experience as a member of the Charlie Spivak, Bunny Berigan and

Woody Herman orchestras. His brother Larry played alto saxophone, and together the Elgart brothers put together a marvelous outfit in 1945 with arrangements by Bill Finegan and Nelson Riddle. Unfortunately, the band failed and soon Les and Larry were free-lancing in New York. In 1951, Larry and arranger-tenor saxophonist Charlie Albertine decided that the time was right to form a new band. They went to Les, got a new group together and made some demo recordings. No label was willing to chance signing a new big band, until manager-music publisher Bill Simon heard the recordings and took them to George Avakian at Columbia records. Avakian loved what he heard, and signed the band soon after. The Elgart brothers' band became a popular favorite at colleges and ballrooms throughout the fifties, and in 1955, it made some of the first live stereo recordings by a big band (these recordings were released in 1995). In 1958, Larry left to start his own orchestra, but he returned to lead the sax section again in the 1960s. Les' band continued to play jobs and do limited touring from his home in Dallas until his death in 1995. The band is still playing in the Dallas area.

Duke Ellington

Theme Songs: East St. Louis Toodle-oo, Take the "A" Train (*featured in this collection*)
Hit Recordings: Solitude (*featured in this collection*), Black and Tan Fantasy, Sophisticated Lady, In a Sentimental Mood, Satin Doll, I Let a Song Go out of My Heart, Come Sunday, and many others.

For millions of music fans around the world, the Duke Ellington Orchestra was the finest big band that was ever organized. He was a composer of many songs that became standards, jazz pieces that are considered classics, orchestral suites, ballets, Broadway shows and religious music performed by all denominations. It is estimated that he composed over 2,000 musical compositions. Edward Kennedy Ellington was born in Washington, D.C. in 1899. (As a teenager a friend of his insisted that each member of their circle had to have a title of nobility, thus Ellington became "Duke.") He began piano at the age of seven, and as a boy was a talented athlete and graphic artist. By the time he graduated from high school he was making a full-time living as pianist, contracter and bandleader. His first trip to New York in 1923 found him working with veteran bandleader Wilbur Sweatman (who could play five clarinets at once), but Ellington was soon back in Washington. He was encouraged to return to New York, and soon formed an ensemble that was hired to play at the Kentucky Club. Exposure and mass popularity was not long in coming, especially since the Ellington band was making recordings and broadcasting nightly from the club. In 1927, Ellington further cemented his band's success by playing at the prestigious Cotton Club in Harlem. By now he was being managed by music publisher Irving Mills, who made the band a national attraction. In 1933, Duke and the band made an unprecedented tour of Europe, where he was treated like royalty. He appeared in Europe frequently before and after the World War II. He continued to record many pieces that were taken up by other bands and singers. In 1939, Ellington met pianist-composer Billy Strayhorn, who not only composed the band's new theme song ("Take the 'A' Train"), but was in effect co-leader of the band and often co-composer of much of the music the band played until Strayhorn's death in 1967. In 1940, two events occured that changed the course of the orchestra. Ellington parted company from Irving Mills, and the bandleader discovered a bassist that became one of the finest musicians to play in a big band, Jimmy Blanton. Blanton played the bass as if it were a melody instrument, forever liberating its function in the jazz ensemble. The ensemble Ellington led from 1940 through 1943 is now considered the best group he ever led, as well as his most fertile compositional period. In 1943, he composed the ground-breaking large-scale concert work "Black, Brown and Beige" for his first appearance at Carnegie Hall. Ellington continued to play his music around the world until his death in 1974, often accompanying major artists and even appearing with symphony orchestras. He was the recipient of many honors and awards throughout his career, culminating with a special 70th birthday party that took place at the White House. His son Mercer has continued leading the ensemble since his death, and Ellington's music continues to be played, studied and enjoyed by people all over the globe. He is now considered to be one of the greatest and most original composers of the twentieth century.

Skinnay Ennis

Theme Song: Got a Date with an Angel *(featured in this collection)*
Hit Recordings: Wishing (Will Make It So)

Robert Ennis started out by playing drums as a student at the University of North Carolina in the Hal Kemp Orchestra. Ennis began singing lead with the band, partially as a joke, but soon became the band's chief draw. After thirteen years with Kemp, he finally left in 1938 to lead his own band, and almost immediately got a regular spot on Bob Hope's "Pepsodent Show." Hope verbally sparred with Ennis during the broadcasts. Being Bob Hope's sidekick on the radio opened many doors, and he quickly got top bookings for his ensemble. Claude Thornhill and Gil Evans wrote some of the band's arrangements. World War II interrupted his musical career with military service. In 1946, he took up bandleading again, and was once again with Bob Hope on the radio for two years, then switched to the "Abbott and Costello Show" for a brief time. The fifties found Ennis and his band touring the country playing top hotels, but basing out of Hollywood. In 1958, he began a permanent booking at the Los Angeles Statler Hilton Hotel, where he remained until his death in 1963. (He died choking on food in a restaurant.)

Dizzy Gillespie

Theme Song: I Waited for You
Hit Recordings: Algo Bueno, Our Delight, Jessica's Day, Groovin' for Nat

John Birks Gillespie was yet another legendary musician that led several wonderful big bands over the years. Born in 1917 in Cheraw, South Carolina, Gillespie gained important experience in the big bands of Teddy Hill and Cab Calloway as solo trumpeter and arranger. He joined the Earl Hines Orchestra just as that ensemble was experimenting with modern jazz in 1943, and became musical director of Billy Eckstine's pioneering modern jazz orchestra in 1944. Gillespie is credited with being one of the most important catalysts in the new style of jazz known (to his chagrin) as 'bebop'. With his leadership abilities and his knowledge of the new music, it was natural that he would be asked to lead his own big band, and in 1945, he assembled a group that appeared as part of a tour called "Hepsations of 1945." Audiences were unsympathetic to the music and Gillespie reluctantly disbanded. He tried again in 1946, and this time the band caught on. This orchestra featured such future jazz stars as Ray Brown, John Lewis, John Coltrane and Kenny Clarke, and was received particularly well in Europe, where the band gave several concerts in 1948. This was the first time that European audiences had ever heard the new jazz. Gillespie found it increasingly hard to keep the band going when he returned to the States, and he began performing more novelty material to appeal to a larger audience. The effort failed, and the band broke up in 1950. Gillespie toured with small groups during the '50s and led an occasional large band for recordings, but he started another big band in 1956 for a U.S. State Department tour of the Middle East. He was encouraged enough to keep the band going until 1958, when low profits and spotty bookings forced him to break it up. Until the end of his life (he died in Englewood, New Jersey, in 1994), he led big bands for special occasions, and always left audiences wanting more.

Benny Goodman
(billed as "The King of Swing")

Theme Songs: Let's Dance, Good-Bye *(both featured in this collection)*

Hit Recordings: It's Been So Long; Goody-Goody; Sing, Sing, Sing; Stompin' at the Savoy; Don't Be That Way; And the Angels Sing; Why Don't You Do Right; Symphony; Jersey Bounce, and many others.

Born in Chicago in 1909, Benjamin Goodman took up the clarinet and played in school bands when he was a boy. He was a professional clarinetist by the time he was in his teens, and was a charter member of the Ben Pollack band in 1926. It was in Pollack's band that he worked with Jack Teagarden, Glenn Miller, Jimmy McPartland, and Victor Young. The jazz community in New York started paying attention to the young clarinetist, and Benny soon found himself a busy free-lancer on clarinet and saxophone. In 1934, his newly-formed big band won a major competition to be featured on the NBC radio show "Let's Dance." It was a huge success, and many music lovers across the country first heard Benny Goodman's new band, playing arrangments by pioneer bandleader Fletcher Henderson. Still, when Benny and band played their new brand of hot swing in live dates across the country in 1935, his music was often met with disdain and downright hostility. The band was reduced to playing stock arrangements in order to hold on to jobs. It was in California, at the Palomar in Pismo Beach on August 21, 1935, to be exact, that the first intimations of a national craze were first experienced. Benny's repertoire of Fletcher Henderson swing met with wild applause for the first time in a public dance engagement in a ballroom. Benny was stunned. There were extended stays at the Congress Hotel in Chicago, with its own weekly radio show ("Camel Caravan") and an appearance in the movie *Big Broadcast of 1937*, but no one realized how popular the band had become until it appeared at the Paramount Theatre in New York on March 3, 1937. On that day, historians say that the swing era

was born. The crowd of teenagers screamed, whistled and stomped in unison. Several couples danced in the aisles. At the end of that first day, there were 21,000 paid admissions, an astonishing number for a school day. The wire services carried the news from coast to coast, and Goodman's band became the hottest attraction in the country. With the addition of such musicians as Teddy Wilson and Lionel Hampton, Goodman succeeded in integrating the ensemble, one of the first major bandleaders to do so. His track record for featuring young talent was extraordinary, and such musicians and singers as Harry James, Charlie Christian, Fletcher Henderson, Gene Krupa, Stan Getz, Helen Ward, Martha Tilton, Helen Forrest, Buddy Greco and Peggy Lee were featured over the years. Goodman's career was made up of firsts. His was the first popular music ensemble to play in Carnegie Hall since 1925, the first American big band to play in Russia since the '20s, and the first jazz musician to 'cross over' into the classical music world. Goodman continued to play to worldwide acclaim until his death in 1986.

Glen Gray & the Casa Loma Orchestra

Theme Song: Smoke Rings *(featured in this collection)*

Hit Recordings: Casa Loma Stomp, Under a Blanket of Blue, Blue Moon, When I Grow Too Old to Dream, Heaven Can Wait, No Name Jive

One of the pioneering big bands of the early 1930s, the Casa Loma Orchestra was led by saxophonist Glen Gray. The band was originally called the Orange Blossoms when it started in Detroit in the mid '20s. It became the first cooperative band, with the members forming a corporation and receiving stock. Gray, who was born Glen Gray Knoblaugh in 1906, became the president, but did not become the front man for the group until 1937. The band made its first recordings in 1929. It accompanied many name singers of the day, and was featured on the "Camel Caravan" radio program. Gene Gifford was responsible for the arrangements, and both the ballads and the up-tempo jump tunes made the band one of the most popular of the pre-swing era. Even though the band was eventually overshadowed by the big new bands of the late 1930s, it continued to be popular with dancers and record buyers. By the mid 1940s, however, with many original members having left, the momentum of the group faded. By the early 1950s, Gray disbanded and went into retirement, but he later returned to music to supervise a series of excellent albums recreating the sounds of the swing era. He died in 1963.

Johnny Green

Theme Song: Hello, My Lover, Goodbye *(featured in this collection)*
Hit Recordings: Two Cigarettes in the Dark, She's a Latin from Manhattan

Green led an excellent big band in between stints as musical director on radio, motion pictures, and as a composer of song hits (among them the classic "Body and Soul"). He was born in New York in 1908. His family wanted him to go into the business world, but he was taken with music as a boy, and studied music while getting a degree in accounting at Harvard University. He composed his first song hit "Coquette" in 1928. Green worked as an arranger for Paramount Pictures in the early '30s, while continuing to compose material for top Broadway performers. He started his orchestra in 1933, and played in the New York area hotels. Green moved to Hollywood, wrote for motion pictures, and eventually accepted the post of musical director of MGM studios. He was a favorite conducter at the Hollywood Bowl, where he appeared regularly until his death in Hollywood in 1989.

Lionel Hampton

Theme Song: Flying Home *(featured in this collection)*
Hit Recordings: Hey! Ba-Ba-Re-Bop, Hamp's Boogie Woogie, Midnight Sun, Rag Mop

Lionel Hampton was born in Louisville in 1909 and moved with his family to Chicago in 1916. He played drums in local bands, and by the late 1920s was living in Culver City, California. It was in recording sessions that Louis Armstrong encouraged Hampton to take up the vibraphone. Lionel soon became the world's foremost performer on this instrument, appearing in many films with Les Hite's band. He even led a big band as early as 1935 in Oregon. But Hampton made a national name for himself when he joined the Benny Goodman Quartet in 1936. When Goodman temporarily disbanded in 1940 due to back problems, Hampton asked to be released from his contract. Goodman let him go, and Hampton put together a unit that was one of the most exciting of the era. It was similar to the Count Basie band, in that the majority of the band's library was made up of 'head arrangements,' which were charts that the band came up with collectively and were written down once the routines were set. Hampton's orchestra was a breeding ground for young talent, including at one time or another Quincy Jones, Clifford Brown, Illinois Jacquet, Benny Bailey, Dexter Gordon, Betty Carter, and Milt Buckner, who wrote many of the band's arrangements. Hampton's band lasted as a permanent unit for many years after most big bands gave up the road, due to its popularity on rock and roll stage shows, as well as many tours around the world. At this writing, he is still playing and touring, in spite of being in ill health.

Coleman Hawkins

Theme Songs: Body and Soul *(featured in this collection)*, Honeysuckle Rose

Primarily known as one of the greatest of tenor sax players in jazz, Coleman Hawkins also had a brief life as a big band leader. He was born in St. Joseph, Missouri, in 1904, and began playing cello at the age of seven, switching to tenor sax two years later, playing professionally by the age of twelve. He atttended high school in Chicago, and college at Washburn University (Topeka). In 1921 he began playing in the pit orchestra at the 12th Street Theater in Kansas City, where blues singer Mamie Smith offered him a touring position, which took him to New York. Hawkins played free-lance with many ensembles over the next years, then settled with Fletcher Henderson for ten years, 1924-1934. His recordings with Henderson attracted much fame and respect. When a Henderson tour of England fell through in 1934, Coleman went ahead on his own, joining some established groups there. Hawkins free-lanced in London and Paris. The progressive recordings made in Europe in the 1930s broke new ground in jazz. Returning to New York in 1941, he formed a nine-piece band of his own, with which he recorded his famous rendition of "Body and Soul," a recording that became a commercial hit. After this success, Hawkins formed a larger big band, but after two years disbanded and instead played with small jazz ensembles for the rest of his life. He was highly acclaimed, and was given every award possible in the field. Hawkins recorded prolifically in the 1950s and 1960s. Alcoholism plagued him in the final years. He died in 1969.

Erskine Hawkins

Theme Song: Tuxedo Junction *(featured in this collection)*
Hit Recordings: Caldonia; Don't Cry, Baby; Tippin' In; After Hours

He was billed as "The Twentieth Century Gabriel," and his was a most powerful and stratospheric trumpet. He also led a wonderful big band. He started the band while in college; it was called the Alabama State Collegians. The band hit the road in 1936 and made the big time with a tune called "Tuxedo Junction." Even though the Glenn Miller band also had a huge hit with the song, Hawkins benefitted greatly from it, and his band did not lack for good play dates and appearances. His main soloists were the Bascomb brothers, Wilbur (trumpet) and Paul (tenor saxophone), and pianist Avery Parrish. Hawkins later put a small group together and played in many clubs across the country. He ended his career playing at the Concord Hotel in the Catskill Mountains in New York, where his lyrical yet powerful horn was a highlight in the lounge. He died in 1993.

Horace Heidt

(Horace Heidt and His Musical Knights)

Theme Song: I'll Love You in My Dreams
Hit Recordings: Gone with the Wind, Ti-Pi-Pin, The Man with the Mandolin, Once in a While, Lovelight in the Starlight, Goodbye Dear I'll Be Back in a Year, I Don't Want to Set the World on Fire *(featured in this collection)*, and many others.

As a child in California, Heidt studied piano at his mother's insistence. More athlete than musician as a teenager, he was injured as a football player at the University of California, and in 1923 began his band at the tender age of 21, which featured tricks by a trained German shepherd. The band played around California for a few years, mainly as a dance band, then toured to New York in the early 1930s, where some important bookings began. The success didn't last, and Heidt headed back to California, and organized a new band. Heidt wound up at the Drake Hotel in Chicago for six years, during which time broadcasts began happening regularly. After the Drake, Heidt headed for the Biltmore Hotel in New York, where he also stayed for six years, and where he also had a radio show. This program, "Pot of Gold," was radio's first listener audience give-away show, and became enormously popular. Heidt kept his band together during the war, and was famous for running an ad for a couple of years in *Billboard* for any qualified, available civilian musician who could swing (they were in short supply during the war). Due to a battle with MCA over his contract, he quit the business in late 1943 and focussed on hotel investments in California. Then, in 1946, Heidt started "The Youth Opportunity Show," an amateur talent contest that toured around for years, became a successful radio show, and made Heidt lots of money. An attempt to convert the radio show to TV failed, and he essentially retired in the mid-1950s. Heidt was really more impresario/front man/organizer than musician, but had a Midas touch.

Fletcher Henderson

Theme Song: Christopher Columbus *(featured in this collection)*
Hit Recordings: Until Today

Fletcher Henderson was one of the most important talents as an arranger in creating the swinging big band style. Benny Goodman, hearing Henderson's band in the 1920s, made the same swing approach popular several years later. Nearly every bandleader owed a stylistic debt of gratitude to Henderson, considered by some to be the "father of the swing era." Unfortunately, Henderson, himself, never experienced much fame and fortune. He led bands from 1923 until the 1950s, and only had nominal national success. Henderson's recordings in the 1920s of his compositions and arrangements created little success. Goodman recorded the same arrangements years later, and made a fortune. Henderson was born in Georgia in 1898, and came to New York in 1920 to go to graduate school in chemistry, but was distracted with a musical career. His first important job was a musical director for an Ethel Waters tour. He formed his own band, which included Coleman Hawkins, and recorded regularly. From 1924 to 1929 Henderson, in residence at the Roseland Ballroom in New York, introduced some major African-American talent (Louis Armstrong, Coleman Hawkins, Joe Smith, and many others), and was musically the envy of every popular musician, black or white, working in New York. After some difficult years, Henderson joined Goodman in 1935 as arranger for a year, then once again had his own band in 1936. This was a hot band with terrific players, but for various reasons it disbanded in 1939, and Henderson once again joined

Benny Goodman. The band he formed in 1941 was musically less successful, though he did manage to keep some kind of ensemble together in residence at the Roseland Ballroom once more during the war. In 1945 he again returned to Goodman. He started a big band one more time in 1950, and died in 1952.

Woody Herman

Metronome

Theme Song: Blue Flame *(featured in this collection)*
Hit Recordings: Woodchopper's Ball *(featured in this collection)*, Blues in the Night, Do Nothin' Till You Hear from Me, Laura, Let It Snow! Let It Snow! Let It Snow!, Sabre Dance, Early Autumn

Woody Herman's band remained innovative and contemporary for nearly fifty years. He was one of the most beloved leaders in the music business who gave many musicians their starts. Above all, his units were consistently excellent. Herman was born in 1913 and was a performer in vaudeville before he joined the Tom Gerun Orchestra. Eventually he played and sang in the internationally famous Isham Jones Orchestra. When Jones decided to disband in 1936, the orchestra re-formed under Woody's leadership. Like the Casa Loma Orchestra, the new Woody Herman orchestra was a cooperative, with the original band members owning stock. They were known originally as "The Band That Plays the Blues," and as such, were only somewhat successful in popularity polls. But the hit record "Woodchopper's Ball" changed everything, and soon the Herman orchestra commanded top engagements. By the early '40s, the band was slowly evolving into a more modern unit with a nod in the direction of the Duke Ellington orchestra. In 1944, with a new contract to record for Columbia records and a new radio program for Old Gold Cigarettes, Woody put together the first of his famous "herds," a sparkling, exciting unit with a group of young musicians with energy to burn — Neal Hefti, Ralph Burns, Sonny Berman, Pete and Conte Candoli, Bill Harris, and Frances Wayne to handle the vocals. Herman's band won every major music poll and performed at Carnegie Hall, premiering a work written especially for it by Igor Stravinsky. Herman disbanded in 1947 at the height of the band's popularity, but he returned later in the year with an even more modern band, which featured Zoot Sims, Stan Getz, Earl Swope, Shorty Rogers and Terry Gibbs. Like most modern orchestras of the time, it lost money and was soon broken up. Herman put together yet another band, and remained on the road for the rest of his life, continuing to discover such new faces as Carl Fontana, Urbie Green, Victor Feldman, Sal Nistico, Bill Byrne, and Frank Tiberi, who currently leads the orchestra. Herman passed away in Los Angeles in 1987.

Harry James

Theme Songs: Ciribiribin (*featured in this collection*), Music Makers
Hit Recordings: You Made Me Love You, Sleepy Lagoon, I Don't Want to Walk Without You, I Had the Craziest Dream, I've Heard That Song Before (*featured in this collection*), I'll Get By, I'm Beginning to See the Light, It's Been a Long, Long Time

Harry James was one of the most versatile trumpet soloists of the swing era, who led a big band for forty years, right up until his death. He was born in Albany, Georgia, in 1916 and trained with his trumpet-playing father, who reportedly was quite rough on the youngster. Before Harry was twenty, he was a soloist with Ben Pollack's band. Recordings of the Pollack band reached Benny Goodman, who asked Harry to join his orchestra. During the three years he was with Goodman he became a major trumpet star, and placed high on music polls. In 1939, James decided to form an orchestra of his own.

Success was elusive for awhile, even though the band featured the vocals of a young Frank Sinatra. In 1941, however, James made the record that really put the band on the map: "You Made Me Love You" (an old song from 1913). Jazz and hot music fans were horrified; one of their favorite soloists was going "corny," adding a string section to boot. But James knew what he was doing to boost his career. His band appeared in many motion pictures and was heard in several radio series. After the war, he dropped the string section and modernized his band, reflecting his love of the music of Duke Ellington and Count Basie. The band continued to be in demand for many years, not only in Hollywood, but in Las Vegas and Lake Tahoe. Toward the end of his life he participated in a tour featuring stars of the swing era. He died in 1983, but his band is still playing for audiences on the road.

Hal Kemp

Theme Song: Got a Date with an Angel (*featured in this collection*)
Hit Recordings: Shuffle Off to Buffalo, In the Middle of a Kiss, There's a Small Hotel, Where or When, It All Comes Back to Me Now, This Year's Kisses (*featured in this collection*)

Kemp's orchestra was another group that began as a college campus band. Hal, born in Marion, Alabama in 1904, attended the University of North Carolina, and put together a band in his senior year. The group caught the attention of bandleader and choral master Fred Waring, who encouraged Hal to bring them to New York. After several difficult years touring, the band hit its stride when it appeared in Chicago's Blackhawk Cafe in 1932. With a few hit records and a great deal of airtime, the band caught on with its unusual staccato trumpet style and smooth clarinet ensembles. The vocals were handled by the band's drummer, Skinnay Ennis, who later started his own successful band. Kemp's arranger and chief architect of the band's style was John Scott Trotter, later known as Bing Crosby's musical director. The band underwent several musical changes in 1939. The staccato trumpets gave way to saxes and warmer big band swing sounds, with the vocalizing of Janet Blair, who later became an actress. On December 19, 1939,

Kemp was traveling from Los Angeles to a job in San Francisco when he was killed in a car crash. Several musicians tried to keep the band going, but by 1941 it was all over.

Stan Kenton

Theme Song: Artistry in Rhythm
Hit Recordings: The Peanut Vendor (El Manisero) *(featured in this collection)*, And Her Tears Flowed Like Wine, Tampico, September Song, Laura

Without doubt, Stan Kenton led one of the most controversial big bands in American music. Either people loved or hated his music, but it was difficult to ignore. Kenton was born in Kansas in 1912, and was raised in California. He gained important experience playing in theatre orchestras, and the dance bands of Everett Hoagland and Gus Arnheim. Arnheim appointed him co-leader of his ensemble in 1937. In 1940, Kenton gathered some of his favorite musicians together to play some arrangements and compositions he was writing. The men encouraged him to put a band together, and after much woodshedding, the band opened in Balboa Beach on Memorial Day, 1941. Word spread quickly about this unusual new organization, and Stan's band soon went out on its first cross-country tour. It signed with Capitol Records and made lots of friends and enemies during the war. In 1946, Stan's was named "Band of the Year" by *Look* magazine, and it gained momentum in many music circles. In 1947, Stan began doing primarily concerts, calling his music "Progressive Jazz." Serious jazz enthusiasts were fascinated, but most of the public only pointed out that "you can't dance to it." He encouraged composers Pete Rugolo and Bob Graettinger to create as they saw fit. He broke up this edition of the band in 1949 after a legendary concert at the Hollywood Bowl, the first big band concert to be televised. In 1950 he returned with a concert orchestra that he called "Innovations in Modern Music," and took the ensemble (which included a large string section) on a tour across the country. In spite of the excellent response, by the end of the second tour, Kenton was heavily in debt. He re-formed a regular size jazz orchestra in 1951, and continued to experiment with new sounds and styles until his death on August 17, 1979. He was a major influence on American music by commissioning music from such important American composers such as Rugolo, Graettinger, Shorty Rogers, Gerry Mulligan, Bill Holman, Johnny Richards and Bill Russo. He also allowed many major improvisational voices to gain valuable experience with his orchestra, such as Art Pepper, Milt Bernhart, Kai Winding, Bob Cooper, Maynard Ferguson, Bud Shank, Bill Perkins, Gabe Baltazar, Lennie Niehaus, and many others. Kenton's music is still studied and performed by high school and college bands, and a worldwide network of fans and musicians organize yearly conventions to honor his contribution to music.

Andy Kirk
(Andy Kirk and His Clouds of Joy)

Theme Song: Until the Real Thing Comes Along *(featured in this collection)*
Hit Recordings: Christopher Columbus, What Will I Tell My Heart, I Won't Tell a Soul

This band was known as Andy Kirk and His 12 Clouds of Joy, and was one of the most popular outfits to come out of Kansas City. Andy Kirk was born in 1898 and got his start with legendary bandleader George Morrison. He was playing in Terence Holder's band when, in 1929, Holder quit the group. Kirk took over, and was soon recording for Brunswick Records. Kansas City was their headquarters for a number of years, but tours of the midwest and east coast were very successful. Most of the band's book was penned by pianist Mary Lou Williams, and she wrote many sparkling original pieces such as "Froggy Bottom" and "Walkin' and Swingin." The band also featured the singing of Pha Terrell, June Richmond and Henry Wells. In later years, it became the starting point for a number of modern jazzmen such as Ken Kersey, Don Byas, Howard McGhee and Fats Navarro. In the early '50s, Kirk led a unit with arrangements by Ray Copeland, but by the end of the decade, he decided to call it quits. He went into real estate, then became a musicians' union official. Kirk died in 1992, one of the most beloved and respected men in the music business.

Gene Krupa

Theme Songs: Apurksody, Starburst

Hit Recordings: There'll Be Some Changes Made *(featured in this collection)*, It All Comes Back to Me Now, High on a Windy Hill, Tonight (Perfidia), Drum Boogie, The Things I Love, Georgia on My Mind, Keep 'Em Flying, Knock Me a Kiss, Old Devil Moon

Krupa was born in Chicago in 1909, and early in life intended to become a minister (he even spent a year in seminary). After some local playing in Chicago, he went to New York in 1929, where he recorded with Red Nichols, Bix Beiderbecke, and other top jazz artists. He signed with Benny Goodman in 1935. Krupa went out on his own in 1938 to form his own band, which always featured his hot drumming. Recordings and steady hotel and ballroom dates came quickly. Gene Krupa believed that black and white musicians should be treated with the same respect. Not only was his one of the first bands to fully integrate, he regularly campaigned for the civil and equal treatment of black musicians out on tour. In 1943 Krupa was arrested in San Francisco on a trumped up charge of marijuana possession. He was sent to jail, and it ended his career for a time. Krupa joined Tommy Dorsey as a drummer, then once again started his own band in 1945, which remained on tour until Krupa's retirement in 1967. He died in 1973. A Hollywood biography, with all the trappings of that genre, was released in 1959, *The Gene Krupa Story.*

Hal Leonard

This regional band is of particular interest to the editors of this book. In 1934 Harold Edstrom and his brother, Ev Edstrom, began a dance band called The Campus Kings in Winona, Minnesota (Minnesota State College for Teachers), along with friend Roger Busdicker. The group played locally, but wanting to play jobs outside the school's area, they searched for another, less collegiate name for the band. The Edstrom brothers thought their conservative Swedish father wouldn't want the family name on a dance band. The amalgamated name was Hal (from Harold) Leonard (Ev's middle name). Personnel changed as players graduated, and the college band eventually ended as everyone went their separate ways. Ev first taught music for two years at the Minnesota State College for Teachers in Winona, and it was during this time that he re-started the Hal Leonard band, as a professional outfit this time, and personally took the name Hal Leonard as bandleader. Ev/Hal was a virtuoso trumpet player who had won a national cornet contest as a youngster. Beginning in about 1936 the new Hal Leonard band began touring the midwest, playing in ballrooms, hotels and theatres, predominantly on the Archer Ballroom circuit, which they shared with Lawrence Welk, among others. In 1941 the band was signed by an important agent who began booking them into more prominent venues. Radio broadcasts, often regional but occasionally coast-to-coast, began to give the band a name. Lawrence Welk was intent on taking his band to the west coast, but was having difficulty getting out of a contract to play an extended engagement at the Trianon Ballroom in Chicago. The ballroom's management wasn't satisfied until the Hal Leonard band was engaged to take the booking. It was a nice break, since the job came with a national radio broadcast. It landed Hal Leonard on the cover of *Billboard* that week. A trademark of the band was a flashy triple tonguing trumpet trio, led by Ev/Hal. Horace Heidt and Fred Waring had both tried to hire the trio. Believe it or not, at one time John Ringling North wanted to put the triple tonguing trumpeters into the circus! By this time Ev Edstrom was known by everyone as Hal Leonard, and when he entered the Navy in 1942, it was as Hal Leonard. Unfortunately, Ev/Hal sustained a back injury while serving and was discharged. Though he had attractive contract offers to play in New York, his injury prevented him from continuing a performing career and the Hal Leonard band was no more. But the name had been established, and when Ev and Hal Edstrom, along with Roger Busdicker, began a music publishing company, initially to publish band music in a swing style for schools — a novel idea at the time —they knew that the name Hal Leonard would mean something to former big band people, many of whom wound up teaching school music. They were certainly right. But that's another story.

Guy Lombardo

(Guy Lombardo and His Royal Canadians)

METRONOME

Theme Song: Auld Lang Syne
Hit Recordings:
Charmaine; Sweethearts on Parade; Goodnight Sweetheart; Paradise; The Last Round-up; Stars Fell on Alabama; Lost; Penny Serenade; Managua, Nicaragua; Boo-Hoo *(featured in this collection)*

In the years before his death in 1977, New Year's Eve was unthinkable without Guy Lombardo's band playing "Auld Lang Syne." He had been playing New Year's Eve engagements ever since the band first played in the United States. Even though its style of music seemed corny to most jazz and hot fans, the Lombardo band must rank as the most commercially successful dance band in the twentieth century, with unmatchable attendance figures over a fifty year career, and sales of over a hundred million records. Lombardo was born in London, Ontario, in 1902 and formed his band in 1923 with his three brothers Carmen, Victor and Lebert. Lombardo was soon heard over the radio in Cleveland and was signed by MCA, soon to be one of the most powerful managing organizations in show business. The band was immediately booked to play in Chicago, and nightly radio broadcasts (many of which Guy paid for himself) brought his sweet style to audiences across the nation. In 1929, the band, now called "Guy Lombardo and His Royal Canadians," played at the Roosevelt Hotel in New York; it would be the band's New York base for almost forty years. When other bandleaders disbanded in the late '40s, the Lombardo band was just as busy as ever, sometimes booked up

to five years in advance for special occasions. The end finally came in Houston, when Guy died of a heart attack in November of 1977. The band continued for awhile under the direction of brother Lebert, but disbanded in the mid '80s. Guy Lombardo is responsible for "Auld Lang Syne," with words by Scottish poet Robert Burns, becoming associated with New Year's Eve, a practice that began in 1929.

Jimmie Lunceford

Theme Song: Uptown Blues
Hit Recordings: T'ain't What You Do (It's the Way That Cha Do It) *(featured in this collection)*, Rhythm Is Our Business, Blues in the Night, Organ Grinder's Swing

One of the most exciting bands that ever appeared on a theatre stage or at a ballroom, the Lunceford band drew clapping and screaming crowds wherever it went. He was born in 1902 and studied music with Wilberforce Whiteman, Paul Whiteman's father. Lunceford graduated from Fisk University in Memphis, and after studying at City College in New York, returned to Memphis to become a gym teacher at a high school. He organized a band that included many of his former students. After extensive road experience, the band became the house orchestra at the famous Cotton Club. It began making some exciting recordings for Decca, and started winning popularity polls by the mid '30s. The band's arrangements were written by Sy Oliver, one of the most influential arrangers of the swing era. It was known primarily as a one-nighter band (as opposed to playing two or three-week engagements in hotels). This was one of the main reasons that, after 1941, Lunceford began losing his best men to other bands. He carried on until he died of a heart attack in 1947.

Billy May

Theme Song: Lean Baby *(featured in this collection)*
Hit Recordings: Charmaine, All of Me, Fat Man Boogie

May originally came from Pittsburgh, Pennsylvania, where he was born in 1916. He studied with the legendary arranging teacher Max Adkins (who also taught Henry Mancini). May brought a batch of arrangements to the Charlie Barnet band for Charlie to try out. Not only did Barnet buy all of the charts, he offered Billy a job with the band. May became the chief arranger, and wrote such best-selling recordings as "Cherokee" and "Pompton Turnpike." After stints arranging for Glenn Miller, Hal McIntire and Alvino Rey, May free-lanced in radio and motion pictures. In 1951, he was hired to write arrangements for an Arthur Murray dance album released on Capitol Records. He wrote four sides with a decidedly two-beat feel similar to the Jimmie Lunceford band, mixing it with "slurping" saxophones and blasting brass. The recordings were so good that Capitol decided to issue them as singles. The singles "took off" and suddenly Billy had the hottest big band sound in the country. After more singles and excellent record sales, Billy was encouraged to go out on the road. He did limited touring during a two-year period, sandwiched in between arranging assignments. Eventually, he sold the band to Ray Anthony, who subsequently hired Sam Donahue to keep it on the road. Billy never regretted his decision to leave the touring life, for he soon built up a high-profile arranging/conducting client list of Nat King Cole, Anita O'Day, Keeley Smith, Ella Fitzgerald, and particularly Frank Sinatra. Along with Nelson Riddle, May created the hard-swinging arranging style that so characterizes the 1950s work of Sinatra's Capitol recordings. At this writing, he is still at it, one of the elder statesmen of American popular music.

Clyde McCoy

Theme Song: Sugar Blues *(featured in this collection)*
Hit Recordings: Smoke Rings, The Goona Goo

A very talented trumpeter who sustained a long musical career based on one hit record, McCoy was born in Kentucky in 1904 and formed a band as early as 1920. He first recorded "Sugar Blues" in 1931, but a later recording made in 1934 was the version that sold over one million copies and catapulted him to success. His band remained popular until World War II, when McCoy and his entire band enlisted in the Navy to entertain the troops. He picked up where he left off after the war, recording "Sugar Blues" yet again in 1946 for the short-lived Vogue label. After retiring in the late '50s, he put together a small Dixieland group that opened at the famous Round Table in New York. The response was so positive that he could be found playing in clubs and concerts for many years after that. He died in Memphis in 1990.

Ray McKinley

Theme Song: Howdy Friends
Hit Recordings: You Came a Long Way from St. Louis *(featured in this collection)*, Civilization (Bongo, Bongo, Bongo)

When Ray McKinley left the band he co-led with Will Bradley, he formed a brand new unit which was well-received. It only lasted a few months, as he lost his best men to the draft. McKinley soon found himself in the Army as well, and he was immediately asked to report to Glenn Miller's Army Air Force Band, one of the legendary pop music ensembles of the war years. McKinley eventually took over leadership of the ensemble when Miller was declared missing in action. After the war, McKinley (who was born in Texas in 1910) put together one of the most progressive of the post-war big bands, with arrangements and compositions by

Eddie Sauter. It took awhile for the band to fully master these pieces, but once they did, the band was the talk of the music business. Unfortunately, its records were poorly recorded, and do not really give an adequate representation of how good the band was. Ray realized that he needed to balance the ensemble's library a bit, so he also featured many novelty songs, most of which he sang himself. The band broke up in 1950, and McKinley free-lanced. In 1956, Helen Miller contacted him to lead a newly re-formed Glenn Miller band. McKinley remained with the organization for nine years, touring all over the world and recording extensively. He remained a popular figure in the music business, and made many appearances in concerts and on television until his death in Florida in 1995.

Glenn Miller

Theme Song: Moonlight Serenade **Hit Recordings:** In the Mood, A String of Pearls, Juke Box Saturday Night, *(all featured in this collection),* Poinciana, Blueberry Hill, Serenade in Blue, Chattanooga Choo Choo, and many others.

When the big band era is discussed, Glenn Miller's band is usually the first band mentioned. He symbolizes the high point of the era of swing music. Equally popular in both the sweet and swing band polls, his popularity continues to be unprecedented to this day. He came from humble Midwest beginnings, born in Clarinda, Iowa, in 1904, but did most of his growing up in Fort Morgan, Colorado, starting his professional musical career playing in the Denver area. He worked as a trombonist in several dance bands in Denver, Colorado, and attended college briefly at the University of Colorado (where he flunked a semester in harmony!). After stints playing with Max Fisher and Georgie Stoll in Los Angeles, Miller joined the Ben Pollack band on the west coast, where he also impressed the other members with his

excellent arrangements. In the Pollack band he worked alongside Benny Goodman and Gil Rodin. He followed the band to New York, and moved there permanently in 1928, free-lanced as a player and arranger in radio and recordings, and studied composition with Joseph Schillinger. Miller played for about a year in the Dorsey Brothers band, then helped the Brit Ray Noble put together his first American group. In 1937 he and his new band went on the road, but success eluded them and the group disbanded by the end of the year. Miller was persuaded to try again, with some financial help from Tommy Dorsey. The band and sound was carefully put together, with a clarinet-lead in the reed section that was distinctive. After a shaky start, the band landed one of the most prestigious engagements a new band could have: the summer season at Glen Island Casino. This engagement, with its many live broadcasts, turned the Miller band into a national sensation. "In the Mood" became a hit about this time. After that the band did turnaway business wherever it played. The band soon acquired a sponsored radio program where it was heard three times a week. Miller featured the arrangements of the brilliant Bill Finegan and Jerry Gray, the vocals of Tex Beneke, Marion Hutton and the Modernaires, and the solo talents of Beneke, Bobby Hackett and Billy May. In 1942, Miller disbanded to become an officer in the Air Force. It was his dream to form a band that would play for the soldiers in England and France, not the traditional military band, but a contemporary swing group. He created one of the great ensembles in popular music, the AEF band, that included a full complement of strings. After a year of propaganda broadcasts, he finally got his wish to bring his band overseas. They played many concerts and broadcasts in England, and made plans to play in France. Miller wanted to go to France before the band arrived, and left England by plane on December 15, 1944. His plane never arrived. The band continued without him, under the direction of Jerry Gray and Ray McKinley. After the war, a new Miller orchestra was assembled and was led by Tex Beneke, but differences between Beneke and the Miller estate forced the estate to pull the library from Beneke, who continued on his own. During the '50s, demand for the Miller sound was so great that Helen, Glenn's widow, asked Ray McKinley to put together a new Glenn Miller orchestra. This group has been together ever since.

Vaughn Monroe

Theme Song: Racing with the Moon

Hit Recordings: There I Go, Is It Love or Is It Conscription?, My Devotion, When the Lights Go On Again (All Over the World), Let's Get Lost, There! I've Said It Again *(featured in this collection)*, Let It Snow! Let It Snow! Let It Snow!, Ballerina, Riders in the Sky, Someday

Born in 1912, Monroe grew up in Massachusetts and formed a band in Boston in 1940. Monroe was a trumpet player (though rarely a soloist) and a big-voiced singer, in addition to his bandleading duties. He had a number one national hit almost immediately in "There I Go," and was regularly on the Hit Parade charts with hit recordings throughout a long career, insuring successful touring. Big success first came in the million-seller hit "There! I've Said It Again" in 1945. A successful radio show in the late 1940s confirmed his popularity. Monroe made several movies and television shows. After 1953, he kept up his performing career as a solo artist only, playing Las Vegas and tours. He died in 1973.

Ben Pollack

Theme Song: Song of the Islands

Hit Recordings: Sweet Sue, Just You, The Beat o' My Heart

As a discoverer of talent, Ben Pollack was matched by few bandleaders, and such men as Benny Goodman, Glenn Miller, Jack Teagarden, Victor Young, Charlie Spivak, Harry James, and Earl Hagen got their starts playing in his band. He was born in Chicago in 1903 and learned the drums as a boy. One of his earliest jobs was playing with the New Orleans Rhythm Kings. In 1925, he formed his first orchestra on the west coast, co-led by saxophonist Gil Rodin. This was one of the premiere big jazz bands of its day, and its recordings and live appearances at colleges made it a big attraction. Gradually, Pollack began to feature himself as a conductor and singer, and Pollack subsequently lost many of his best players. He led another excellent orchestra in the mid-'30s, but by 1935 the band left him as a group and re-formed under the leadership of Bob Crosby. Pollack led bands on and off for the rest of his life, as well as involving himself in many other ventures (such as a talent agency and a record label, Jewell), but they failed. In failing health and in financial straits, he hung himself in his Palm Springs home in 1971.

Johnny Richards

Theme Song: Young at Heart *(featured in this collection)*

Hit Recording: Estoy Cansado

Richards was an innovative, respected arranger in the jazz community, one of the best educated in popular music, and led two sparkling, innovative ensembles. He was born in 1911 and studied many instruments as a boy. He was musical director of a theatre in Philadelphia by the time he was 17. The young man studied arranging while attending Syracuse University. He was in England writing film scores in the early '30s, and also studying composition with Ralph Vaughan Williams. Returning to the U.S., he studied with Arnold Schoenberg in Los Angeles. While in Hollywood, he was Victor Young's personal musical assistant at Paramount Studios and Decca Records. In 1940 he put together his first big band, playing the tenor saxophone solos himself. The music was progressive for its time, jazz-oriented, and too unusual for most listeners. Johnny, disillusioned and broke, disbanded in 1945. During the '40s he wrote for Charlie Barnet and Boyd Raeburn. He was arranger/conductor for the first ever use of jazz soloist with strings, a recording date with Dizzy Gillespie, but the records were never released. By 1952, he was a staff composer for Stan Kenton, a union that served both men very well. Richards wrote many important pieces for Kenton over the years. It was the success of Richards' suite "Cuban Fire" that led Kenton to assist Richards in forming another band of his own. Johnny led this orchestra on and off until his death, supplementing his income by arranging for Ben Webster and many other jazz and pop greats. He died of cancer in 1968.

Jan Savitt

(Jan Savitt and His Top 26 Hatters)

Theme Songs: Quaker City Jazz, It's a Wonderful World
Hit Recordings: 720 in the Books, Make Believe Island, Where Was I?, Sugarfoot Stomp *(featured in this collection)*

Born in Russia in 1912 to a father who led the Imperial Regiment Band under Czar Nicholas II, the Savitt family immigrated to Philadelphia before Jan was two years old. He began violin at six, and at fifteen was invited by Stokowksi to play with the Philadelphia Symphony. Savitt soon switched his interest to popular music, and was fronting a band, doing arrangements and playing, on the road by 1936. Savitt's arranging was in a "shuffle style" that some say originated with him. Success in important bookings, broadcasts, recordings, and even motion pictures soon came. Following the trend of the postwar period, Savitt scaled down his ensemble and moved to California. He died suddenly at the age of thirty-six in 1948.

Artie Shaw

Theme Song: Nightmare
Hit Recordings: Star Dust *(featured in this collection),* Goodnight Angel, Begin the Beguine, They Say, Thanks for Ev'rything, Frenesi, and many others.

Shaw rivalled Goodman as the greatest swing era clarinetist. Critics have often stated that Artie Shaw had the best big band of the entire swing era. Born in New York City in 1910, he grew up in Connecticut. Young Artie was playing sax and clarinet in dance bands in his teens. He first toured with Johnny Cavallaro's dance band, and wound up in Cleveland, where he worked from 1926 to 1929, and where he also discovered classical music, particularly Debussy and Stravinsky. Shaw headed to New York in 1929, "studied" with Willie Smith, and free-lanced until forming his first group in 1936 for a concert, presenting an original composition ("Interlude in B-flat"). This band, with unusual orchestration and music, did not catch on, and Shaw disbanded in 1937. That same year he formed a conventional swing band, and soon recorded the big hit "Begin the Beguine." He made a movie in 1940 (*Second Chorus*). Despite success and fame, Shaw, not comfortable with a career as a celebrity in popular music, disbanded in 1941. He briefly had another ensemble, of a more serious jazz nature, before service in the Navy began in 1942. Shaw was asked to form a band while in the service, and led this throughout the Pacific war zone. Out of the service, he organized an excellent new jazz band in 1944. Over the next decade he maintained a big band on occasion, was active as a jazz musician and composer, and continued to perform. He retired in 1954 at the age of 44. More intellectual than performer by nature, Shaw disliked the grind of playing his hits night after night. In the 1970s he revealed that he had not played the clarinet for twenty years. Shaw was known as a champion for integrating bands. He was married eight times. He once again organized a big band for touring in 1983.

Claude Thornhill

Theme Song: Snowfall *(featured in this collection)*
Hit Recordings: Loch Lomond, A Sunday Kind of Love, For Heaven's Sake (Let's Fall in Love)

When it came to both romantic sounds and innovative stylings, the Thornhill band was *it* for many listeners. Claude was born in Indiana in 1910, and he might have been a gifted classical pianist if he did not turn to popular music instead. He studied at Cincinnati Conservatory and at the University of Kentucky. Thornhill began as a teenager playing and arranging for bands in the Indiana/Ohio area. He eventually went to New York, where he joined the Ray Noble orchestra in 1934, and free-lanced as an accompanist and arranger. He was musical director of the Skinnay Ennis band on the west coast for a number of years, where he first met arranger Gil Evans. Thornhill moved back to New York in 1940 and assembled an orchestra that was the talk of the music world by the time it ended its engagement at the Glen Island Casino in 1941.

Thornhill stressed warm ensemble sounds and dynamic control that made the ensemble exciting and yet soothing to listen and dance to. By 1942 Evans and arranger Bill Borden had joined the band, and the band, now larger, was even stronger. World War II intervened, and Thornhill joined the Navy, putting together special shows and organizing units to entertain the troops. He reformed after the war, and this edition is the one that is so beloved by musicians and modern jazz fans. It featured Evans' scores once again, and the band played such modern jazz pieces as "Anthropology," "Yardbird Suite," and "Elevation." It was this band that later influenced the ensemble that Miles Davis led in 1948-50 (the "Birth of the Cool" ensemble). By 1950, Thornhill had lost many of his best musicians, but he continued leading a band until his death in 1965. The Thornhill band is more popular now than it was in 1947, with many reissues of his recordings and live performances of Gil Evans' classic scores.

Chick Webb

Theme Song: I May Be Wrong (But I Think You're Wonderful)
Hit Recordings: Stompin' at the Savoy *(featured in this collection)*, A-Tisket, A-Tasket

Webb was the idol of such drummers as Gene Krupa and Buddy Rich, and had the distinction of defeating the Benny Goodman Orchestra in a "battle of swing" at the Savoy Ballroom in Harlem. Chick was born in Baltimore in 1909, and played drums with several bands until he came to New York in 1924. Duke Ellington helped the Webb band become established when Chick started it in 1926. Webb's band regularly filled the Apollo Theatre in Harlem and the Savoy when it appeared there. Many fine musicians played with him at one time or another, including Johnny Hodges, Benny Carter, John Kirby and Edgar Sampson, who wrote "Stompin' at the Savoy" and "Don't Be That Way." But Webb's biggest star was undoubtedly Ella Fitzgerald, who won the amateur talent contest at the Apollo Theatre several times. Bardu Ali of the Webb band saw her there and recommended that she join the band. Initially unenthusiastic, Webb grew to love her, as did the rest of the group. After Webb died in 1939, Ella led the band for several years until she went out as a single performer.

Ted Weems

Theme Song: Out of the Night **Hit Recordings:** Heartaches *(featured in this collection)*, Somebody Stole My Gal, The Man from the South, I Wonder Who's Kissing Her Now

The Weems band provides one of the most incredible stories in American show business. Weems started his band in 1923 at the University of Pennsylvania (he was born in 1901 and grew up in Philadelphia), and it was popular in its midwestern tours. Weems moved the band to Chicago to get radio work. The band was heard nationally, and built a solid reputation over the next years. In 1932 Weems got his first sponsored radio show. He began recording, and had solid hits from the late '20s until 1942. At various times he featured the whistling of Elmo Tanner and, in the 1930s and 1940s, the singing of two future stars, Perry Como and Marilyn Maxwell (named Marvel Maxwell in her Weems days). Weems conducted a band in the merchant marines during the war, and once again resumed his dance band after the war. Then in 1947 a strange thing happened. A recording of the song "Heartaches," which Weems had made in 1933 (and which the publisher hated), was rediscovered years later by a disc jockey in North Carolina. He plugged it continuously until other radio hosts picked it up and made it into a huge national hit, selling over two million copies, and Weems, unexpectedly, found himself the biggest attraction in the music business. He and his band remained on the road making personal appearances. Weems, himself, became a disc jockey in the 1950s, first in Memphis, then later in Dallas, though he kept doing occasional band tours. He passed away in 1963.

Lawrence Welk

Theme Song: Bubbles in the Wine
Hit Recordings: The Moon is a Silver Dollar, Don't Sweetheart Me

Welk was born on a farm in North Dakota in 1904, and studied the accordion. Soon he was playing dances and functions locally. He formed his first band, "Welk's Novelty Orchestra" in 1925, and soon began broadcasting daily from Yankton, South Dakota. The response was so positive that Welk started playing many ballrooms in the Dakotas. Welk's distinctive style of light dance music, called "champagne music" because of its bubbly sound, was popular for many years in the Chicago area and the midwestern ballrooms, and broadcasting regionally from the Trianon Ballroom in Chicago. (Critics called his style "Mickey Mouse.") He played his first engagements on the west coast in 1945, but had little success there initially, returning to his bread-and-butter work in the midwest. Then, in 1951, Welk was booked in the Aragon Ballroom in southern California, which began broadcasting a local television show. This successful local show was signed in 1955 by ABC television, which booked the show as a summer replacement. The show was not expected to go past the summer, but Welk knew his audience well and gave them what they wanted. The show became one of the biggest success stories in television, lasting sixteen years on the network. It was finally cancelled, not due to poor ratings, but because the executives at ABC felt that his audience was too old. Welk quickly found a syndication company that would distribute the show to local stations, and was soon on more stations across the U.S. than he had been on ABC. The show remained in production until 1982. Welk died in 1990, leaving an estate worth millions, including a resort bearing his name, and a record company that is still in operation. Though he was an unlikely candidate, Welk was the only bandleader to have longterm success on television.

Bob Wills

Theme Song: San Antonio Rose
Hit Recordings: Big Beaver, Worried Mind, We Might as well Forget It

Wills was the main proponent of "western swing" to most music listeners, and indeed, that distinctive style is his most important contribution to American music. But in the early '40s, he led his biggest and most swing/jazz-oriented ensemble. He was born in Texas in 1905. He learned the mandolin and guitar to accompany his father and grandfather, both fiddlers. From the very beginning, he was not only exposed to country and folk music, but to blues and jazz. He took up the violin and put together a band that played dances and medicine shows. In 1931 the band had its own radio show under the sponsorship of Light Crust Flour; they became known as The Light Crust Doughboys. In 1933, after numerous disagreements with the sponsor, Bob left and formed another band called the Playboys. By 1935, the band, now relocated to Tulsa, Oklahoma, had its own show on station KVOO. Its reception was overwhelming, and it soon had more offers for dances than it could handle. By 1938 Wills kept adding men to create a more swing/jazz-oriented orchestra, and its records during this time featured exciting hot swing instrumentals. The onset of the war forced Wills to cut the band down. Wills was one of the first country artists to champion electric guitars and mandolins, and caused quite a stir at traditional country establishments like The Grand Ole Opry. But since Wills never considered his band a country group, he went on playing his mix of jazz, blues, fiddle tunes and music for dancing. By the mid-'50s Wills' poor health was slowing him down, and in 1962, he suffered a heart attack. A second heart attack two years later caused him to break the band up. He was inducted into the Country Music Hall of Fame in 1968. He died in 1975. Recent reissues of his classic recordings prove that his music is more popular than ever.

THE BIG BAND ERA

Featured Vocalists with the Big Bands

A very selective list of only some of the most prominent artists. Thousands of singers sang with the bands between the 1920s and 1950s. Typically, a vocalist would only stay with a band a brief time, at most a few years.

Singer	Band	Singer	Band
Ivie Anderson	Earl Hines Duke Ellington	Skinnay Ennis	Hal Kemp
Gene Barry	Teddy Powell	Dale Evans	Anson Weeks
Vivian Blaine	Al Kavelin	Alice Faye	Rudy Vallee
Art Carney	Horace Heidt	Ella Fitzgerald	Chick Webb
June Christy	Stan Kenton	Helen Forrest	Benny Goodman Artie Shaw Harry James
Buddy Clark	Wayne King Freddy Martin	Georgia Gibbs	Artie Shaw
Rosemary Clooney	Tony Pastor	Edyie Gorme	Tex Beneke
Dorothy Collins	Raymond Scott	Betty Grable	Hal Grayson Ted Fiorito
Russ Columbo	Gus Arnheim		
Perry Como	Ted Weems	Merv Griffin	Freddy Martin
Doris Day	Barney Rapp Les Brown Bob Crosby	Connie Haines	Tommy Dorsey Harry James
Gloria DeHaven	Muzzy Marcelino Bob Crosby Jan Savitt	Dick Haymes	Tommy Dorsey Benny Goodman Harry James
Mike Douglas	Kay Kyser	Woody Herman	Isham Jones
Ray Eberle	Glenn Miller	Harriet Hilliard	Ozzie Nelson
Billy Eckstine	Earl Hines	Billie Holiday	Count Basie Artie Shaw

Kitty Kallen

Helen Forrest

Singer	Band		Singer	Band
Lena Horne	Noble Sissle Charlie Barnet Artie Shaw		Helen O'Connell	Jimmy Dorsey Austin Wylie
Helen Humes	Count Basie Harry James		Anita O'Day	Bob Crosby Woody Herman Stan Kenton Gene Krupa
Betty Hutton	Vincent Lopez		Patti Page	Benny Goodman
June Hutton	Ina Ray Hutton			
Herb Jeffries	Duke Ellington Earl Hines		The Rhythm Boys (Bing Crosby, Al Rinker, Harry Barris)	Gus Arnheim
Kitty Kallen	Jimmy Dorsey Harry James Jack Teagarden		Shirley Ross	Hal Grayson Gus Arnheim
The King Sisters	Horace Heidt Alvino Rey		Jimmy Rushing	Count Basie
Dorothy Lamour	Herbie Kay		Jane Russell	Kay Kyser
Abbe Lane	Xavier Cugat		Dinah Shore	Leo Reisman
Frances Langford	Jimmy Dorsey		Frank Sinatra	Tommy Dorsey Harry James
Peggy Lee	Benny Goodman		Jo Stafford	Tommy Dorsey
Art Lund	Benny Goodman		Kay Starr	Joe Venuti Charlie Barnet
Gordon MacRae	Horace Heidt			
Tony Martin	Anson Weeks		Martha Tilton	Hal Grayson Benny Goodman
Marilyn Maxwell	Buddy Rogers Ted Weems		Mel Torme	Ben Pollack
Johnny Mercer	Richard Himber Paul Whiteman		Sarah Vaughan	Billy Eckstine Earl Hines
The Modernaires, with Paula Kelly	Charlie Barnet Glenn Miller		Frances Wayne	Charlie Barnet
Vaughn Monroe	Austin Wylie		Joe Williams	Count Basie
Russ Morgan	Freddy Martin		Eileen Wilson	Les Brown

Helen O'Connell

Tommy Dorsey and
Frank Sinatra

Martha Tilton and
Benny Goodman

Ray Anthony
THE MAN WITH THE HORN

Lyric by EDDIE DeLANGE
Music by JACK JENNEY, BONNIE LAKE
and EDDIE DeLANGE

Desi Arnaz
CUBAN PETE

By JOSÉ NORMAN

Gus Arnheim
SWEET AND LOVELY

Words and Music by GUS ARNHEIM,
CHARLES N. DANIELS and HARRY TOBIAS

41

Charlie Barnet

CHEROKEE
(INDIAN LOVE SONG)

Words and Music by
RAY NOBLE

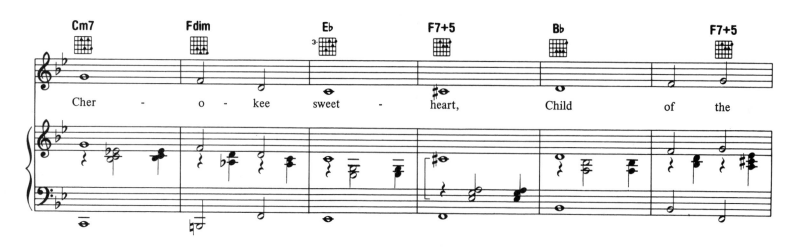

Bunny Berigan

I CAN'T GET STARTED WITH YOU
from ZIEGFELD FOLLIES

Words by IRA GERSHWIN
Music by VERNON DUKE

Count Basie

ALRIGHT, OKAY, YOU WIN

Words and Music by SID WYCHE
and MAYME WATTS

Moderately, with rhythm

Will Bradley

BEAT ME DADDY, EIGHT TO THE BAR

Words and Music by DON RAYE,
HUGHIE PRINCE and ELEANOR SHEEHY

In a dink-y honk-y tonk-y vil-lage in Tex - as,

there's a guy who plays the best pi-an-o by far. ___

He can play pi-an-o an-y way that you like ___ it,

Les Brown
LEAP FROG

Music by JOE GARLAND

MCA music publishing

Les Brown

SENTIMENTAL JOURNEY

By BUD GREEN,
LES BROWN and BEN HOMER

Les Elgart
BANDSTAND BOOGIE
from the Television Series AMERICAN BANDSTAND

Words by BARRY MANILOW and BRUCE SUSSMAN
Music by CHARLES ALBERTINE

Frankie Carle

SUNRISE SERENADE

Lyric by JACK LAWRENCE
Music by FRANKIE CARLE

Xavier Cugat
MY SHAWL

English Lyric by STANLEY ADAMS
Spanish Lyric by PEDRO BERRIOS
Music by XAVIER CUGAT

Jimmy Dorsey
AMAPOLA
(PRETTY LITTLE POPPY)

By JOSEPH M. LACALLE
New English Words by ALBERT GAMSE

Tommy Dorsey

LET'S GET AWAY FROM IT ALL

Words and Music by TOM ADAIR
and MATT DENNIS

Tommy Dorsey

MARIE

from the Motion Picture THE AWAKENING

Words and Music by
IRVING BERLIN

Sonny Dunham

MEMORIES OF YOU

Lyrics by ANDY RAZAF
Music by EUBIE BLAKE

Billy Eckstine
A COTTAGE FOR SALE

Words by LARRY CONLEY
Music by WILLARD ROBISON

Duke Ellington
SOLITUDE

Words and Music by DUKE ELLINGTON,
EDDIE DE LANGE and IRVING MILLS

Duke Ellington
TAKE THE "A" TRAIN

Words and Music by
BILLY STRAYHORN

Skinnay Ennis

GOT A DATE WITH AN ANGEL
from FOR THE LOVE OF MIKE

Words by CLIFFORD GREY and SONNY MILLER
Music by JACK WALLER and JOSEPH TURNBRIDGE

Benny Goodman

LET'S DANCE

Words by FANNY BALDRIDGE
Music by GREGORY STONE and JOSEPH BONINE

GOOD-BYE

Benny Goodman

Words and Music by
GORDON JENKINS

Glen Gray and the Casa Loma Orchestra
SMOKE RINGS

Words by NED WASHINGTON
Music by H. EUGENE GIFFORD

Johnny Green

HELLO, MY LOVER, GOODBYE

Words by EDWARD HEYMAN
Music by JOHNNY GREEN

Lionel Hampton

FLYING HOME

Music by BENNY GOODMAN and LIONEL HAMPTON
Lyric by SID ROBIN

Coleman Hawkins
BODY AND SOUL

Words by EDWARD HEYMAN, ROBERT SOUR and FRANK EYTON
Music by JOHN GREEN

Erskine Hawkins

TUXEDO JUNCTION

Words by BUDDY FEYNE
Music by ERSKINE HAWKINS, WILLIAM JOHNSON and JULIAN DASH

123

124

Horace Heidt

I DON'T WANT TO SET THE WORLD ON FIRE

Words and Music by SOL MARCUS,
BENNIE BENJAMIN and EDDIE SEILER

Fletcher Henderson

CHRISTOPHER COLUMBUS

Lyric by ANDY RAZAF
Music by LEON BERRY

Woody Herman

BLUE FLAME

Lyric by LEO CORDAY
Music by JAMES NOBLE and JOE BISHOP

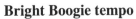

Woody Herman
WOODCHOPPER'S BALL

By JOE BISHOP
and WOODY HERMAN

Bright Boogie tempo

Harry James

CIRIBIRIBIN

Based on the original melody by A. PESTALOZZA
English Version by HARRY JAMES and JACK LAWRENCE

Harry James

I'VE HEARD THAT SONG BEFORE

from the Motion Picture YOUTH ON PARADE

Lyric by SAMMY CAHN
Music by JULE STYNE

Hal Kemp

THIS YEAR'S KISSES

from the 20th Century Fox Motion Picture ON THE AVENUE

Words and Music by
IRVING BERLIN

I did-n't cry when ro-mance was through,

I looked a-round for some-bod-y new.

Since my ro-mance I've

Mis - ter Moon __ a - bove. ____

This year's crop of kiss - es is not for me, __

__ for I'm still wear - ing last __ year's

love.

love. ____

Stan Kenton

THE PEANUT VENDOR
(EL MANISERO)

English Words by MARION SUNSHINE and L. WOLFE GILBERT
Music and Spanish Words by MOISES SIMONS

Gene Krupa

THERE'LL BE SOME CHANGES MADE

from ALL THAT JAZZ

Words by BILLY HIGGINS
Music by W. BENTON OVERSTREET

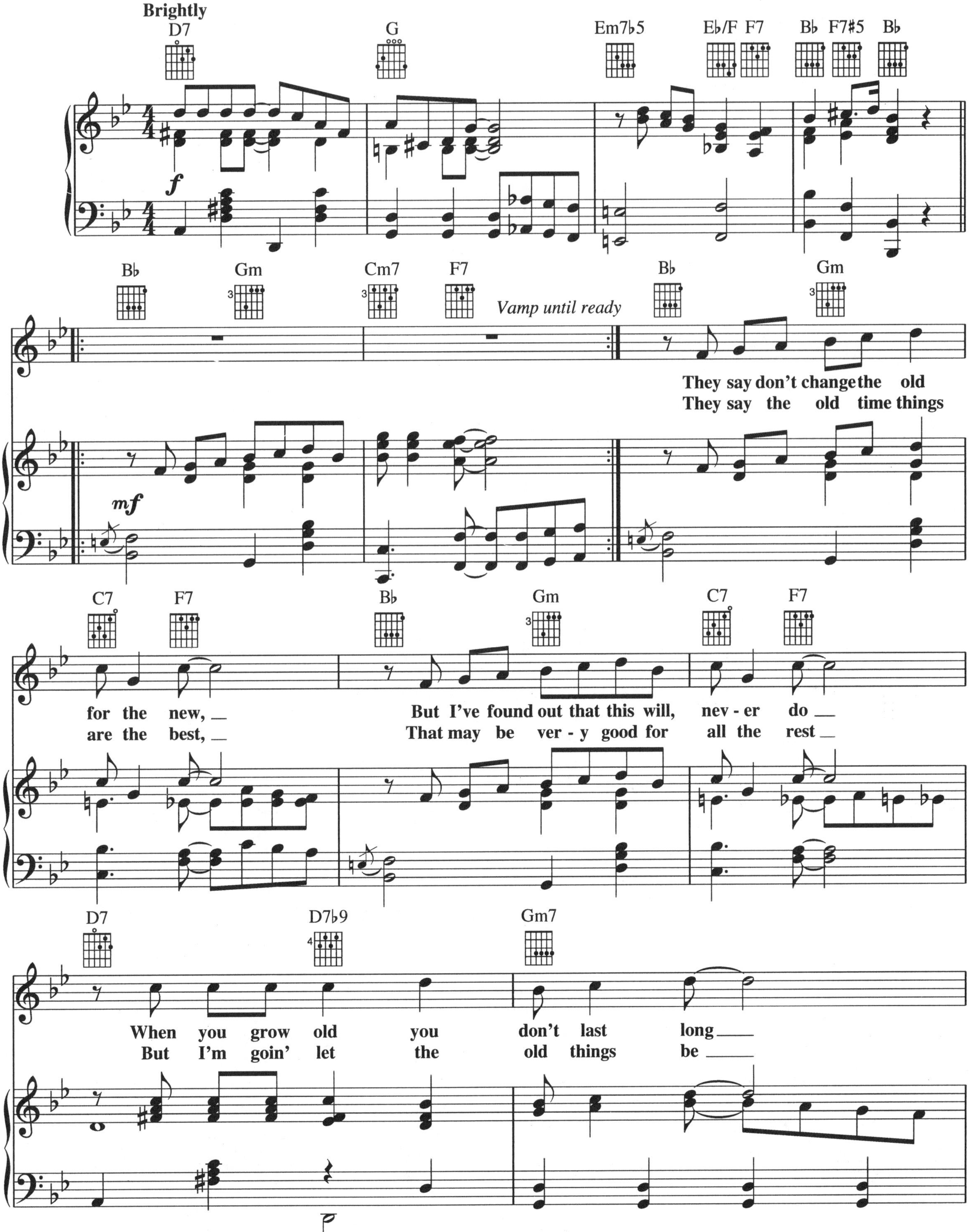

Brightly
D7
G
Em7♭5
E♭/F F7
B♭ F7♯5 B♭
f
B♭
Gm
Cm7
F7
Vamp until ready
B♭
Gm
mf
They say don't change the old
They say the old time things
C7
F7
B♭
Gm
C7
F7
for the new, But I've found out that this will, nev - er do
are the best, That may be ver - y good for all the rest
D7
D7♭9
Gm7
When you grow old you don't last long
But I'm goin' let the old things be

fade a - way, ___ There'll be some chang - es

made to - day __ There'll be some chang - es made.

Additional Choruses

1. There's a change in your manner
   And a change in your way
   There was time once when you was O.K.
   You once said you saved ev'ry kiss for my sake
   Now you're giving all the girls an even break
   I'm gonna send out invitations to the men I know
   'Cause you're gettin' colder than an Eskimo
   I must have my lovin' or I'll fade away
   There'll be some changes made to-day
   There'll be some changes made.

2. For there's a change in your manner
   There's a change in your style
   And here of late you never wear a smile
   You don't seem to act like a real lover should
   You can't thrill your mamma if you're made of wood
   I gotta have a man who loves me like a real live Skeik
   With a tasty kiss that lingers for a week
   I'm not over sixty so it's time to say
   There'll be some changes made to-day
   There'll be some changes made.

3. For there's a change in your squeezin'
   There's a change in your kiss
   It used to have a kick that I now miss
   You'd set me on fire when you used to tease
   Now each time you call I just sit there and freeze
   You had a way of making love that made a hit with me
   One time you could thrill me but it's plain to see
   You're not so ambitious as you used to be
   There'll be some changes made by me
   There'll be some changes made.

4. There's a change in the weather
   There's a change in the sea
   From now on there'll be a change in me
   I'm tired of working all of my life
   I'm gonna grab a rich husband and be his wife
   I'm going to ride around in a big limousine
   Wear fancy clothes and put on plenty of steam
   No more tired puppies, will I treat you mean
   There'll be some changes made to-day
   There'll be some changes made.

5. For there's a change in your manner
   There's a change in your smile
   From now on you can't be worth my while
   I'm right here to tell you with you I'm thru
   Your brand of lovin' will never do
   I'm gettin' tired of eating just butter and bread
   I could enjoy a few pork chops instead
   You know variety is the spice of life they say
   There'll be some changes made to-day (I'll get mine)
   There'll be some changes made.

Additional Choruses by WILSON and RINGLE
Copyright © 1924 by Edward B. Marks Music Company
Copyright Renewed

Andy Kirk

UNTIL THE REAL THING COMES ALONG

Words and Music by MANN HOLINER, ALBERTA NICHOLS,
SAMMY CAHN, SAUL CHAPLIN and L.E. FREEMAN

Guy Lombardo

BOO-HOO

Lyric and Music by EDWARD HEYMAN,
CARMEN LOMBARDO and JOHN JACOB LOEB

Jimmie Lunceford

T'AIN'T WHAT YOU DO
(IT'S THE WAY THAT CHA DO IT)

Words and Music by SY OLIVER
and JAMES YOUNG

Moderately

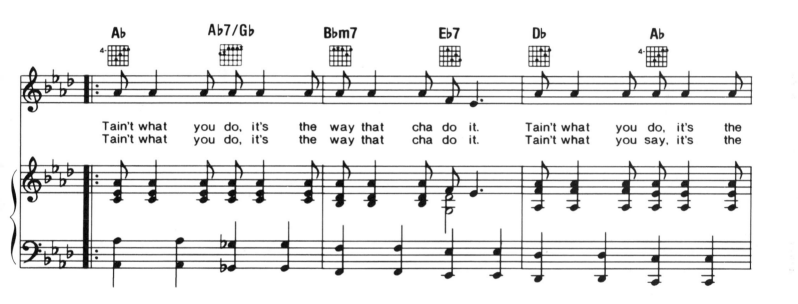

Tain't what you do, it's the way that cha do it. Tain't what you do, it's the
Tain't what you do, it's the way that cha do it. Tain't what you say, it's the

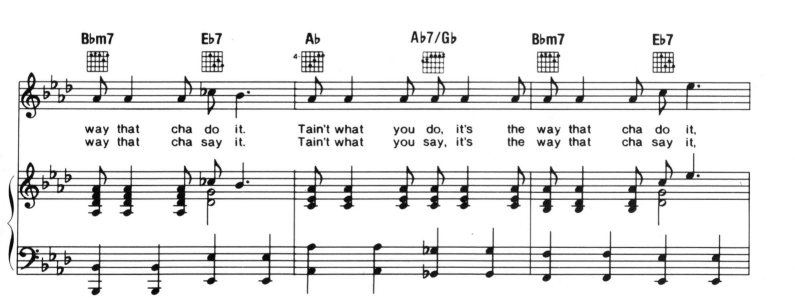

way that cha do it. Tain't what you do, it's the way that cha do it,
way that cha say it. Tain't what you say, it's the way that cha say it,

MCA music publishing

Billy May
LEAN BABY

Lyric by ROY ALFRED
Music by BILLY MAY

Moderate Swing

Lyrics:

My lean ba-by {tall / small} and thin, __ five feet sev-en of bones and skin. __ But when {she / he} tells me may-be {she __ / he __} loves me, __ I feel as {mel-low as a fel-low can be. __ / whirl-y as a girl-y can be. __} {She's / He's} so skin-ny, {she's __ / he's __}

Clyde McCoy
SUGAR BLUES

Words by LUCY FLETCHER
Music by CLARENCE WILLIAMS

Moderate Blues tempo

Have you   heard __ these   blues
I   just   love __ sweet   food,

that I'm going to sing   to
puts me in   a   nice   sweet

you?
mood.

When you   hear them,
When I'm   like that,

they will thrill you through and
you will nev - er   find   me

Ray McKinley

YOU CAME A LONG WAY FROM ST. LOUIS

Words by BOB RUSSELL
Music by JOHN BENSON BROOKS

Glenn Miller

JUKE BOX SATURDAY NIGHT

Words by AL STILLMAN
Music by PAUL McGRANE

Glenn Miller
A STRING OF PEARLS

Words by EDDIE DeLANGE
Music by JERRY GRAY

Moderately Bright

Glenn Miller
IN THE MOOD

By JOE GARLAND

Vaughn Monroe

THERE! I'VE SAID IT AGAIN

By DAVE MANN
and REDD EVANS

Johnny Richards
YOUNG AT HEART

Words by CAROLYN LEIGH
Music by JOHNNY RICHARDS

Artie Shaw
STAR DUST

Words by MITCHELL PARISH
Music by HOAGY CARMICHAEL

...And now the pur-ple dusk of twi-light time

steals a-cross the mead-ows of my heart.

High up in the sky the

lit-tle stars climb,

al-ways re-mind-ing me that

Jan Savitt

SUGAR FOOT STOMP

Lyric by WALTER MELROSE
Music by JOE OLIVER

Chick Webb
STOMPIN' AT THE SAVOY

Words and Music by BENNY GOODMAN, EDGAR SAMPSON,
CHICK WEBB and ANDY RAZAF

Ted Weems
HEARTACHES

Words by JOHN KLENNER
Music by AL HOFFMAN

You said you loved me just as I love you, ____

And I be-lieved it all; ____

Claude Thornhill
SNOWFALL

Lyrics by RUTH THORNHILL
Music by CLAUDE THORNHILL

The Greatest Songs Ever Written

The Best Ever Collection
Arranged for Piano, Voice & Guitar

150 Of The Most Beautiful Songs Ever
Over 400 pages of slow and sentimental ballads, including: Come In From The Rain • Edelweiss • The First Time Ever I Saw Your Face • For All We Know • How Deep Is Your Love • I Have Dreamed • I'll Be Seeing You • If We Only Have Love • Love Is Blue • Red Roses For A Blue Lady • Songbird • Summertime • Unchained Melody • Yesterday, When I Was Young • Young At Heart • many more.
00360735 ....$19.95

The Best Big Band Songs Ever
69 of the greatest big band songs ever, including: Ballin' The Jack • Basin Street Blues • Boogie Woogie Bugle Boy • The Continental • Don't Get Around Much Anymore • In The Mood • Let A Smile Be Your Umbrella • Marie • Moonglow • Opus One • Satin Doll • Sentimental Journey • String Of Pearls • Who's Sorry Now.
00359129 ....$15.95

The Best Broadway Songs Ever
Over 65 songs in all! Highlights include: All I Ask Of You • As Long As He Needs Me • Bess, You Is My Woman • Bewitched • Camelot • Climb Ev'ry Mountain • Comedy Tonight • Don't Cry For Me Argentina • Everything's Coming Up Roses • Getting To Know You • I Could Have Danced All Night • I Dreamed A Dream • If I Were A Rich Man • The Last Night Of The World • Love Changes Everything • Oklahoma! • Ol' Man River • People • Try To Remember • and many more!
00309155 ....$17.95

The Best Christmas Songs Ever
A collection of 72 of the most-loved songs of the season, including: Blue Christmas • The Chipmunk Song • Frosty The Snow Man • A Holly Jolly Christmas • Home For The Holidays • I'll Be Home For Christmas • Jingle-Bell Rock • Let It Snow! Let It Snow! Let It Snow! • Parade Of The Wooden Soldiers • Rudolph, The Red-Nosed Reindeer • Santa, Bring Back My Baby (To Me) • Silver Bells • Suzy Snowflake • Toyland.
00359130 ....$17.95

The Best Country Songs Ever
Over 65 songs, featuring: Always On My Mind • Behind Closed Doors • Could I Have This Dance • Crazy • Daddy Sang Bass • D-I-V-O-R-C-E • Forever And Ever, Amen • God Bless The U.S.A. • Grandpa (Tell Me 'Bout The Good Old Days) • Help Me Make It Through The Night • I Fall To Pieces • Mammas Don't Let Your Babies Grow Up To Be Cowboys • Stand By Your Man • Through The Years • and more.
00359135 ....$16.95

The Best Easy Listening Songs Ever
A collection of 75 mellow favorites, featuring: All Out Of Love • Can't Smile Without You • (They Long To Be) Close To You • Every Breath You Take • Eye In The Sky • How Am I Supposed To Live Without You • I Dreamed A Dream • Imagine • Love Takes Time • Piano Man • The Rainbow Connection • Sing • Vision Of Love • Your Song.
00359193 ....$15.95

The Best Jazz Standards Ever
77 of the greatest jazz hits of all time, including: April In Paris • Body And Soul • Don't Get Around Much Anymore • I Got It Bad And That Ain't Good • I've Got You Under My Skin • It Don't Mean A Thing (If It Ain't Got That Swing) • Love Is Here To Stay • Misty • Out Of Nowhere • Satin Doll • Unforgettable • When I Fall In Love • and many more.
00311641 ....$17.95

The Best Love Songs Ever
A collection of 66 favorite love songs, including: The Anniversary Song • (They Long To Be) Close To You • Endless Love • Here And Now • Just The Way You Are • Longer • Love Takes Time • Misty • My Funny Valentine • So In Love • You Needed Me • Your Song.
00359198 ....$17.95

The Best Movie Songs Ever
Over 70 songs, including: Alfie • Beauty And The Beast • Born Free • Endless Love • Theme From "Jurassic Park" • Moon River • Somewhere Out There • Tears In Heaven • A Whole New World • and more.
00310063 ....$19.95

The Best Rock Songs Ever
70 songs, including: All Day And All Of The Night • All Shook Up • Ballroom Blitz • Bennie And The Jets • Blue Suede Shoes • Born To Be Wild • Boys Are Back In Town • Every Breath You Take • Faith • Free Bird • Hey Jude • Lola • Louie, Louie • Maggie May • Money • We Got The Beat • Wild Thing • more!
00490424 ....$16.95

The Best Songs Ever – Revised
Over 70 must-own classics, including: All I Ask Of You • Body And Soul • Crazy • Endless Love • In The Mood • Love Me Tender • Memory • Moonlight In Vermont • My Funny Valentine • People • Satin Doll • Save The Best For Last • Somewhere Out There • Strangers In The Night • Tears In Heaven • A Time For Us • The Way We Were • When I Fall In Love • You Needed Me • and more.
00359224 ....$19.95

The Best Standards Ever
Volume 1 (A-L)
72 beautiful ballads, including: All The Things You Are • Bewitched • Don't Get Around Much Anymore • Getting To Know You • God Bless' The Child • Hello, Young Lovers • It's Only A Paper Moon • I've Got You Under My Skin • The Lady Is A Tramp • Little White Lies.
00359231 ....$15.95

Volume 2 (M-Z)
72 songs, including: Makin' Whoopee • Misty • Moonlight In Vermont • My Funny Valentine • Old Devil Moon • The Party's Over • People Will Say We're In Love • Smoke Gets In Your Eyes • Strangers In The Night • Tuxedo Junction • Yesterday.
00359232 ....$15.95

FOR MORE INFORMATION, SEE YOUR LOCAL MUSIC DEALER, OR WRITE TO:

HAL•LEONARD™
CORPORATION
7777 W. BLUEMOUND RD. P.O. BOX 13819 MILWAUKEE, WI 53213

Prices, contents and availability subject to change without notice. Not all products available outside the U.S.A.

0995